ENGLISH SKILLS
BY OBJECTIVES

BOOK TWO

ENGLISH SKILLS BY OBJECTIVES

BOOK TWO

Grammar and Usage

This book is derived from
an instructional program
created by the

AMERICAN PREPARATORY INSTITUTE

Central Texas College, Killeen

CAMBRIDGE Adult Education
Prentice Hall Career & Technology
Englewood Cliffs, New Jersey 07632

Cambridge gratefully acknowledges the advice and contributions of the following adult educators who reviewed the draft version of this book:

Donna Amstutz, Chicago Urban Skills Institute, Chicago, Illinois.

Janet Moore, Coordinator, A.B.E. Section, Birmingham City Schools, Birmingham, Alabama.

Denise Schultheis, Springfield Community Schools, Springfield, Ohio.

Nancy Sullivan, Jersey City Learning Center, Jersey City, New Jersey.

Project Editor:	James Fina
Production Manager:	Arthur Michalez
Managing Editor:	Eileen Guerrin
Contributing Editors:	Vicki Tyler, Gina Doggett

Dictionary excerpt on page 104. With permission. From *Webster's New World Dictionary,* Compact School & Office Edition.
Copyright © 1982 by Simon & Schuster, Inc.

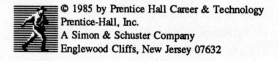

© 1985 by Prentice Hall Career & Technology
Prentice-Hall, Inc.
A Simon & Schuster Company
Englewood Cliffs, New Jersey 07632

Printed in the United States of America

10   9   8   7

ISBN   0-8428-0214-2   NB2I

Prentice-Hall International (UK) Limited, *London*
Prentice-Hall of Australia Pty. Limited, *Sydney*
Prentice-Hall Canada Inc., *Toronto*
Prentice-Hall Hispanoamericana, S.A., *Mexico*
Prentice-Hall of India Private Limited, *New Delhi*
Prentice-Hall of Japan, Inc., *Tokyo*
Simon & Schuster Asia Pte. Ltd., *Singapore*
Editora Prentice-Hall do Brasil, Ltda., *Rio de Janeiro*

CONTENTS

TO THE STUDENT

The three-book series, ENGLISH SKILLS BY OBJECTIVES, is designed to help you develop the skills that you need to write effectively. BOOK ONE, GRAMMAR FUNDAMENTALS, introduced the grammar, or structure, of the English language. In studying from it, you learned to identify the parts of speech and the parts of a sentence. This is BOOK TWO, GRAMMAR AND USAGE. In it you will learn more about the parts of speech and how to use them correctly. You will study the various forms of nouns. You will learn to recognize the parts of sentences, and how to use different verb forms correctly. You will find out how to use adjectives, adverbs, and phrases as modifiers, and you will practice using modifiers to make sentences more accurate and interesting. You will also learn how to recognize common sentence patterns, and how to choose the correct pronouns. When you complete your studies in this book, you will understand how to use the parts of the English language correctly in speaking and in writing.

The title of this series, ENGLISH SKILLS BY OBJECTIVES, means that the material to be learned is broken into smaller "objectives" or goals for you to accomplish. Here's how the program works:

Pretest—Take the Pretest to find out what English skills you need to work on. Don't worry about any questions whose answers you don't know. This book will help you learn the answers. Check your answers in the separate Answer Key and then turn to the Skills Correlation Chart on pages 14 and 15 in the text. The Chart lists the pages in this book that you should study so that you can answer the questions you missed.

Skill Units—This book contains 10 Skill Units. Each Skill Unit is divided into smaller units called "Subskills." Each Subskill focuses on a specific part of an English language skill, thus allowing you to learn one thing at a time. You will always know what you are to learn and how you will learn it. Each Subskill starts with an objective explaining what language activity you will be able to perform after you finish the Subskill. At the end of each Subskill, there is an EXERCISE for you to complete to see how well you understand the material. If you need additional practice, you complete a SUPPLEMENTAL EXERCISE that also includes a review of the Subskill. You can use the Subskill exercises for review at any time. At the end of each Skill Unit, there is a SELF-CHECK. Completing this exercise allows you to check your understanding of all that you have learned in the unit. Because the Self-Check has no time limit, you can take your time thinking about each question before you answer.

Posttest—Take the Posttest to review your performance in all the skills in ENGLISH SKILLS BY OBJECTIVES, BOOK TWO. Then use the Skills Correlation Chart to interpret your score on the Posttest. You will be able to go back and review those Skill Units and Subskills in which you need more practice.

When you complete this book, you will know a great deal about the correct way to use words. Then you will be ready for the last book in the ENGLISH SKILLS BY OBJECTIVES series. BOOK THREE, WRITING SKILLS, will help you build on the skills you already have to write effectively in English.

LIST OF ABBREVIATIONS

The following lists the abbreviations used in the example sentences in this book:

AV	action verb
Adj	adjective
Adv	adverb
DO	direct object
HV	helping verb
IO	indirect object
LV	linking verb
MV	main verb
O Prep	object of a preposition
P Pro	predicate pronoun
PA	predicate adjective
PN	predicate noun
Prep Phrase	prepositional phrase
S	subject
V	verb

Pretest
GRAMMAR AND USAGE

Before you begin working on this book, take the following test. The test will help you find out how much you already know about grammar and usage. The test will also show you which parts of the book you should study most.

The test is divided into ten parts, one part for each unit in the book. You may want to take the test all at once or one unit at a time, depending on what you and your instructor decide. When you complete the test, check your answers starting on page 1 in the Answer Key for Book Two. Then turn to the Skills Correlation Chart on pages 20 to 22 in this book and circle the numbers of any questions you miss. The chart will show you which parts of this book cover the English skills that give you the most trouble. You should study the skill units that contain the questions you miss on the test.

Skill Unit 1: Recognizing and Capitalizing Nouns

Part A. Underline all the nouns you find in the following sentences.

EXAMPLE: The **man** was rewarded for his **patience**.

1. Please pay close attention to the instructor.

2. Grammar is my favorite subject.

3. My daughter wants a new swimsuit for her birthday.

4. Her friendship helped me through a difficult time in my life.

Part B. Rewrite each sentence, capitalizing all the proper nouns.

EXAMPLE: My best friend, ramon sanchez, lives in tucson, arizona.
          My best friend, **R**amon **S**anchez, lives in **T**ucson, **A**rizona.

5. Which street will take me to the clarks' house more directly, whittier boulevard or chelten avenue?

6. Of all the people in my division at delta manufacturing company, malcolm and barbara are the most dependable workers.

1

7. He took several classes at the martin college of business and atlanta community college.

_____

_____

_____

8. Unfortunately, marilla can't arrive before thursday.

_____

_____

_____

Part C. Read the following sentences carefully. Underline all the noun determiners you find and circle the nouns they signal.

EXAMPLE: The (mother) frowned at her (son), whose (hands) were still dirty.

9. Margot's only chance was to find a new adviser.

10. Raoul looked frantically through his pockets, but he found only a comb, a few coins, and a grocery receipt.

11. That show was the worst comedy Edna and Tim had ever seen together.

12. Because of the snarled traffic, Alphonse and Pierre missed the first 20 minutes of the soccer game.

Part D. Many of the nouns in the following sentences have special noun endings. Underline all the special noun endings you find.

EXAMPLE: The establish**ment** of a recrea**tion** fund was the next step.

13. This facility does not have all the equipment it needs for the job.

14. The woman's fondness for her nephew showed in the lavish attention she paid to him.

15. Were Mr. Hardy's assurances enough to relieve Marie's anxiety?

16. Our instructor explained the major applications of the theory and its potential usefulness.

Part E. Rewrite the following sentences, capitalizing all proper nouns.

EXAMPLE: Last summer on our vacation we drove all the way across the south from beaumont to atlanta.
Last summer on our vacation we drove all the way across the South from Beaumont to Atlanta.

17. Did aunt penny call father before she left for albany?

_____

_____

18. I went to see dr. michaels yesterday.

_____

_____

19. He told me i should go west on highway 54 after i leave portland, maine.

_____

_____

20. I asked mother to go with us to hear the boston pops.

_____

_____

Skill Unit 2: Using the Plural and Possessive Forms of Nouns

Part A. Write the plural form for each noun given below.

EXAMPLE: bench **benches**

1. tax _____

2. letter _____

3. city _____

4. sheep _____

5. knife _____

6. woman _____

Part B: Fill in the first blank in the following exercise using the singular possessive form of the noun. Fill in the second blank using the plural possessive form.

EXAMPLE: goose the **goose's** beak
geese the **geese's** beaks

7. man the _____ car
men the _____ cars

8.	wolf	the	_____	howl
	wolves	the	_____	howls
9.	baby	the	_____	bottle
	babies	the	_____	bottles
10.	boy	the	_____	bicycle
	boys	the	_____	bicycles
11.	witness	the	_____	testimony
	witnesses	the	_____	testimonies

Part C.   In the spaces provided, write each noun you find in the following sentences and state whether it is singular, singular possessive, plural, or plural possessive in form.

EXAMPLE: Julie's car was parked at her parents' house.
        <u>Julie's—**singular possessive,** car—**singular,** parents'—</u>
        <u>**plural possessive,** house—**singular.**</u>

12.   Mark Ross's uncles all live in Denver.

_____

_____

13.   The children's new teacher is strict.

_____

_____

14.   My nieces' husbands are all very tall.

_____

_____

15.   The children have finally arrived for Thomas's birthday party.

_____

_____

16.   The members' dues were collected and the roll was called.

_____

_____

Part D.   Underline the correct form of the word to complete each of the following sentences.

EXAMPLE: The   (Welch's, Welches, **Welches'**)   car broke down.

17.   My   (father's, fathers, fathers')   friends all like to fish.

18.   The   (Boy Scouts, Boy Scout's, Boy Scouts')   meet every Thursday night.

19.   This   (knife's, knives, knives')   blade is badly bent.

20.   The   (womens, women's, womens')   room is at the end of the hall.

Skill Unit 3:   Reviewing Verbs

Part A.   Divide each sentence into two parts by drawing a line between the complete subject and the complete predicate. Then underline the simple subject once and the verb twice.

EXAMPLE: My oldest **aunt**|**traveled** to San Francisco recently.

1.   The trees swayed in the high winds.

2.   Vice President Carla Summers opened the meeting.

3.   My favorite food is lasagne.

4.   He lives next door to us.

Part B.   In each pair of sentences below, the underlined word is used once as a noun and once as a verb. Write N next to the sentence with the underlined noun and V next to the sentence with the underlined verb.

EXAMPLE: **N**   Fred filed the reports carefully.
              V   My sister reports to work at 8 a.m.

5.   _____   The police officer shot the rabid dog.

      _____   The nurse gave the child a shot.

6.   _____   Will the judge reverse her decision?

      _____   Put the car into reverse and back up carefully.

7.   _____   It makes no sense to me.

      _____   They can sense the danger.

8.   _____   The call came at 4:00 in the morning.

      _____   Please call me tonight.

Part C. Each of the following sentences contains a verb phrase. For each sentence, do the following:

- Underline all the words in the verb phrase.
- Write <u>HV</u> above the helping verbs.
- Write <u>MV</u> above the main verb of each sentence.

Review your work to be sure you have completed each step.

                        HV   HV MV
EXAMPLE: They **might have left** already.

9.   We are going to Cincinnati on Wednesday.

10.   Karina will be needing your help.

11.   Martin had just gone to bed.

12.   You should call your sister.

Part D. Each of the following sentences contains a linking verb or linking verb phrase. Underline the verb or verb phrase in each sentence.

EXAMPLE: The trip **was becoming** more difficult in the later stages.

13.   I am a careful driver.

14.   The test seemed easy to the students.

15.   I have been very discouraged.

16.   He has become one of our best customers.

Part E. Each of the following sentences contains a form of the verb <u>to be</u>. For each sentence, do these steps:

- Underline the verb.
- Decide if the form of <u>to be</u> is used as a linking verb or if it is used as a helping verb in a verb phrase. Write <u>LV</u> in the blank if it is used as a linking verb and write <u>HV</u> if the form of <u>to be</u> is used as a helping verb.

Review your work to make sure you have completed each step.

EXAMPLE: I <u>am</u> terrified of heights.   **LV**

Henry <u>was helping</u> me with my taxes.   **HV**

17.   The plane will be taking off at 7:00 a.m.   _____

18.   They were very good friends.   _____

19.   You should have been certain.   _____

20.   I am driving Jake to the store.   _____

Part F. The following sentence pairs use the same words as linking verbs and action verbs. Read the sentence pairs carefully. Decide which sentence uses the word as an action verb and write <u>AV</u> in the space provided. Write <u>LV</u> next to the sentence in which the word is used as a linking verb.

EXAMPLE: This food smells funny. **LV**

Martin smells a rat. **AV**

21. Martha always <u>feels</u> the tomatoes carefully. _____

Herman <u>feels</u> tired today. _____

22. Sarah <u>grew</u> used to living on the farm. _____

The farmer <u>grew</u> corn and barley. _____

23. My mother <u>looked</u> at several watches. _____

They all <u>looked</u> expensive. _____

Skill Unit 4: Using Verb Tenses Correctly

Part A. Fill in the blanks with the correct present tense form of the verb indicated in parentheses.

EXAMPLE: Kevin _____**wishes**_____ he had enough time to go swimming, but _____**relies**_____ on television for entertainment most evenings. (wish, rely)

1. On Sunday, Hugo always _____ the football game and _____ popcorn. (watch, eat)

2. Eric _____ always late for appointments and never _____ time for lunch. (be, have)

3. Tony always _____ home after work and _____ dinner for the children. (rush, make)

Part B. Fill in the blanks with the correct past tense form of the verb indicated.

EXAMPLE: The newborn _____**fretted**_____ and _____**cried**_____ all morning. (fret, cry)

4. I _____ at home last night and _____ a call from an old friend. (be, get)

5. Caroline _____ and _____ on the icy sidewalk. (slip, fall)

6. On our vacation, we _____ to Montana, where we _____ relatives and _____ on their generous hospitality. (go, visit, rely)

Part C. Rewrite each of the following sentences twice. First change the verb to the future tense using <u>will</u>. Next change the verb to the future tense using <u>be + going to</u>.

EXAMPLE: Karl and Janet had a great time.
<u>Karl and Janet will have a great time.</u>
<u>Karl and Janet are going to have a great time.</u>

7. I am very patient.

_____

_____

8. This shirt matches my blue slacks.

_____

_____

_____

_____

9. They hurried to catch the last bus.

_____

_____

_____

_____

Part D. Each of the following sentences is written in the past tense. On the lines provided, rewrite each sentence in the present perfect, the past perfect, and the future perfect tenses.

EXAMPLE: PAST: Julia went to her aunt's apartment.

PRES. PERF.: <u>Julia has gone to her aunt's apartment.</u>

PAST PERF.: <u>Julia had gone to her aunt's apartment.</u>

FUT. PERF.: <u>Julia will have gone to her aunt's apartment.</u>

10. PAST: We finished the job before 2:00 p.m.

PRES. PERF.: _____

_____

PAST PERF.: _____

_____

FUT. PERF.: _____

11. PAST: I had only an hour's sleep.

PRES. PERF.: _____

_____

PAST PERF.: _____

_____

FUT. PERF.: _____

_____

12. PAST: They went to bed already.

PRES. PERF.: _____

_____

PAST PERF.: _____

_____

FUT. PERF.: _____

_____

Skill Unit 5:   Using Progressive Forms and Irregular Verbs

Part A.   In each of the following sentences, underline the correct helping verb of each pair in parentheses. Then fill in the blank with the progressive form of the verb in parentheses under the blank.

EXAMPLE: During the last game, the players (were, **have been**)

___**committing**___   many fouls.
(commit)

1.   I (have, am) _____ the dishes now.
(wash)

2.   In December, Alexandra (have been, will have been)
_____   in New York for one year.
(live)

3.   For his vacation, Don (had been, will be) _____
new clothes.   (buy)

4.   This morning the dog (was, has been) _____ out
the window.   (stare)

5.   Tom was unhappy because he (had been, will have been)
_____   for his clothes to dry for a long time.
(wait)

Part B.   Fill in the blanks in the following with either the past or the past participle form of the verb in parentheses.

EXAMPLE: Mary Ellen _____**lost**_____ her keys last night. (lose)

6.   The china doll fell and _____ into a million pieces.
(break)

7.   I have _____ Sue for a long time. (know)

8.   Last night, Dave thought he _____ a flying saucer. (see)

9.   Kristen _____ me for not calling her. (forgive)

10.   What _____ he say to you? (do)

Part C.   Above each of the following sentences are the principal parts of one or two verbs. In each blank, write the verb form that correctly completes each sentence.

EXAMPLE: lie lay lain   lay laid laid

Maggie had _____**lain**_____ down for a short nap.
Peter had ____**laid**____ his keys on the kitchen table.

11.   rise rose risen   raise raised raised

Jorge _____ the window.

They had all _____ from their seats.

12.   sit sat sat   set set set

Terry always _____ the table at dinnertime.

They _____ next to us at the picnic.

13.   let let let   leave left left

Richard _____ the twins stay up an extra hour.

I am sure we _____ before midnight.

Skill Unit 6:   Identifying Adjectives and Using Them Correctly

Part A.   Underline all the adjectives you find in the following sentences.

EXAMPLE: The **snaggle-toothed**, **freckle-faced** **little** boy smiled when he saw his teacher.

1.   Gudrun bought a new housecoat and some furry, red slippers.

2.   The contented children played with the bright, colorful toys.

3.   My five boisterous cousins raced through the crowded room.

4.   Quang cooked another delicious Vietnamese meal for us.

5.   Those terrifying stories frightened young Billy.

Part B.   Underline all the adjectives you find in the following sentences.

EXAMPLE: The puppy, though **wet** and **cold**, looked **healthy**.

6.   Alberto's three sons seem friendly and outgoing.

7.   The worried look on the mother's face told me something frightening might happen.

8.   The new day found us tired but excited about the long climb to the cloud-covered top of the mountain.

9.   My hard-driving Costa Rican friend devoted himself to his demanding job.

10.   Peter's young wife felt ignored and unloved.

Part C. Change the words given in parentheses into adjectives by adding one of the following endings: <u>ible</u>, <u>able</u>, <u>ic</u>, <u>ous</u>, <u>ious</u>, <u>itious</u>, <u>less</u>, <u>al</u>, <u>ive</u>, and <u>ful</u>. Be sure to make any necessary spelling changes. Use a dictionary if you are in doubt.

EXAMPLE: It was the **<u>sensible</u>** thing to do.   (sense)

11. Martin is a very _____ dancer. (grace)

12. Brenda had an _____ day. (act)

13. The decision was _____ to all. (agree)

14. This tool is not very _____. (use)

15. She thought the lesson was _____. (repeat)

Part D. Fill in the blanks using the comparative and superlative forms of the adjectives given.

EXAMPLE: funny   This movie is ____**funnier**____ than the one we saw last month.
　　　　　　　 This is the ____**funniest**____ movie I have ever seen.

16. thin   This material is _____ than I expected.
　　　　　 It is the _____ I have ever used.

17. early   We got up _____ than usual this morning.
　　　　　　 It's the _____ I've ever gotten up.

18. good   The food here is much _____ than I thought.
　　　　　 It's the _____ I've ever eaten.

19. exciting   Tonight's game is _____ than last week's.
　　　　　　　 This game is the _____ game I have ever watched.

20. bad   The baby's cough is _____ than it was yesterday.
　　　　　 It is probably the _____ cough he has ever had.

Skill Unit 7: Identifying Adverbs and Using Them Correctly

Part A. For each of the following sentences, do the following:
- Underline the adverbs you find.
- Draw an arrow to the word each adverb modifies.

- On the blank following the sentence, write <u>How?</u>, <u>When?</u>, <u>How often?</u>, <u>Where?</u>. or <u>How much?</u> to show what question the adverb answers about the word it modifies.

Review your work to make sure you have completed each step.

EXAMPLE: Rudolph stretched **lazily.** **How?**

1. The dog barked noisily. _____

2. Our guests will arrive tomorrow. _____

3. Pam and her sister are quite late. _____

4. We go there for ice cream. _____

Part B. Expand the following sentences using the adverbs given in parentheses. Several different placements may be correct.

EXAMPLES: The dog jumped onto the table. (suddenly)
Each of the following answers is correct:

> <u>Suddenly the dog jumped onto the table.</u>
> <u>The dog suddenly jumped onto the table.</u>
> <u>The dog jumped suddenly onto the table.</u>
> <u>The dog jumped onto the table suddenly.</u>

The solution was to pay $5. (only—There were no other solutions.)
The following is the only correct answer:

> <u>The only solution was to pay $5.</u>

5. The baby reached for the candy. (quickly)

_____

_____

6. The letter carrier is late with the mail this morning. (extremely)

_____

_____

7. I regretted going to see her father. (never—I didn't ever regret going to see him.)

_____

_____

8. I regretted going to see her father. (never—I regretted that I didn't ever go to see him.)

_____

_____

Part C.   Use the adverb form of the underlined adjective used in the first sentence to complete the second sentence in each set.

EXAMPLE: Fred was very _____ busy _____ with a new project.
            Fred worked _____ **busily** _____ on his new project.

9. We had to take a _____ late _____ flight to Miami.
    We arrived in Miami very _____ last night.

10. His stare was _____ cold _____ as ice.
    He stared at me _____ .

11. The bride's mother was _____ frantic _____ before the wedding.
    The bride's mother rushed around _____ before the wedding.

Part D.   Fill in the blanks with the comparative and superlative forms of the adverb given.

EXAMPLE: quickly   The days seem to pass _____ **more quickly** _____ in summer than in winter.
                     The last beautiful days of Indian summer are gone the _____ **most quickly** _____ of all.

12. carefully   My friend Jake drives _____ than I do.
                Of all my friends, Jake drives the

                _____ .

13. well   Susan paints _____ than Renate.
           Of all the art students, she paints the

           _____ .

14. readily   The baby laughs _____ than his sister.
              Of all the children, he laughs the _____ .

Part E.   Read each of the sentence pairs below. Underline the word in parentheses that correctly completes each sentence.

EXAMPLE: Margaret yelled (angry, **angrily**) at the intruders.
            She certainly felt (**angry**, angrily) about the mistake.

15. I felt (bad, badly) about that.
    I felt the door (careful, carefully).

16. The music sounds too (loudly, loud) to me.
    The whistle blows (loud, loudly) at noon.

17. Gustave looked (sad, sadly) at the old picture.
    Gustave looked (sad, sadly) after the wedding.

Part F.   Underline the word in parentheses that correctly completes each sentence.

EXAMPLE: They don't have (anywheres, **anywhere**) to stay tonight.

18. He was   (real, really)   pleased to receive the award.

19. Jenny   (seldom, seldom ever)   comes to see us anymore.

20. Your idea works   (real, really)   (good, well).

Skill Unit 8:   Using Prepositional Phrases as Modifiers

Part A.   Read the following sentences and do these steps:

- Underline all the prepositional phrases you find.

- Circle each preposition.

- Write OP above the object of the preposition.

Review your work to make sure you have completed each step.

EXAMPLE: (In) the summer, we have picnics (in) the park.

1. We went to the park by way of the turnpike.

2. A cool breeze was blowing over the lake.

3. Suddenly a dark cloud moved in front of the sun.

4. Rain fell without warning.

5. We ran for shelter under the trees.

6. We laughed in spite of the rain.

7. After the rain, we walked down the path to our car.

8. Behind us, a rainbow arched across the sky.

Part B.

Part I.   Read the following sentences and do these steps:

- Underline all the prepositional phrases you find.

- Draw an arrow to the word each phrase modifies.

- In the blank, write <u>adjective</u> if the phrase modifies a noun or pronoun. Write <u>adverb</u> if the phrase modifies the verb.

Review your work to make sure you have completed each step.

EXAMPLE: We walked   **in the park** .   **adverb**

9. Two people hurried aboard the plane.   _____

10. The child without a coat looks cold.   _____

11. George waited behind the curtain.   _____

12. My report is on top of yours.   _____

13. Turn left at the next light.   _____

14. The white car near the corner is mine.   _____

Part II. In some of the following sentences, it is clear what the prepositional phrases are describing. In others, the placement of the phrases has confusing or even humorous results. If the meaning of the sentence is clear, write C in the blank. If the meaning is not clear, rewrite the sentence, changing the position of the prepositional phrase.

EXAMPLE: We can see many distant stars with powerful telescopes.
With powerful telescopes, we can see many distant stars.

15. In the bottom of her bag, Julie was looking for loose change.

_____

_____

16. In spite of her fear of heights, Carla climbed to the top of the monument.

_____

_____

17. Tony asked for an assistant with his hands on his hips.

_____

_____

18. Between the cracks in the sidewalk, the children found several pretty wildflowers growing.

_____

_____

19. After the blizzard, the roads were closed for three days.

_____

_____

20. In the nest, Herman tried to see the baby birds.

_____

_____

Skill Unit 9:   Identifying Simple Sentence Patterns

Part A.   Each of the following sentences fits one of these basic sentence patterns:
Subject + Action Verb   (S + AV)
Subject + Action Verb + Direct Object   (S + AV + DO)
Subject + Action Verb + Indirect Object
  + Direct Object   (S + AV + IO + DO)
Identify the sentence type by writing the sentence pattern formula in the blank following the sentence.

EXAMPLE: They left immediately.   **S + AV**

1.   Martin ate two pizzas and a submarine sandwich.

   _____

2.   My aunt gave me the antique necklace.   _____

3.   Bernice and Joe called today.   _____

4.   Dad and Lou caught fifteen fish at the lake today.

   _____

5.   Uncle Hank sends my sister and me birthday cards.

   _____

6.   Nelson reads quietly in his room every afternoon.   _____

Part B.   Each of the following sentences fits one of these basic sentence patterns:
Subject + Action Verb   (S + AV)
Subject + Action Verb + Direct Object   (S + AV + DO)
Subject + Action Verb + Indirect Object
  + Direct Object   (S + AV + IO + DO)
Subject + Linking Verb + Predicate Noun   (S + LV + PN)
Subject + Linking Verb + Predicate
  Adjective   (S + LV + PA)
Identify the sentence type by writing the pattern formula in the blank after each sentence.

EXAMPLE: We are good friends with his family.   **S + LV + PN**

7.   Nancy is an excellent basketball player. _____

8.   She will be giving me a lesson next week. _____

9. ʌMy son felt feverish last night after dinner. _____

10.ʌ I felt his forehead with my hand. _____

11. They are leaving for Pittsburgh in the morning.

_____

12. They are happy about the move. _____

13. This trip has really been interesting and educational.

_____

14. The trip to the farm was a real adventure. _____

Part C. Read each of the following sentences carefully and do these three steps:

- Rewrite the sentence in the usual order (subject + verb) on the lines provided.
- If the sentence has a subject that is understood, put the understood subject in parentheses in your rewritten version.
- Write S above each subject and V above each verb.

Review your work to be sure you have completed each step.

EXAMPLE: Give the apple to your sister.

        S   V
    (You) give the apple to your sister.

15. Are we going to the park on Saturday?

_____

16. Stop that noise!

_____

17. There is too much food on your plate.

_____

18. Will we see you again?

_____

19. At the edge of the field stands an old oak tree.

_____

_____

20. Here are your shoes.

_____

Skill Unit 10:   Using Pronouns Correctly

Part A.   Underline the correct pronouns to complete each sentence.

EXAMPLE: (**He,** Him)   and   (**I,** me)   asked Shirley and   (she, **her**) to go to the movies with   (we, **us**)   on Saturday.

1.   Andy told   (they, them)   and   (I, me)   about the sidewalk sale at the shopping center.

2.   The representatives chosen were Cheryl and   (her, she).

3.   (We, Us)   lucky gentlemen are going with   (they, them)   to the dance.

4.   Bertil is not as tall as   (I, me).

Part B.   Underline the correct pronouns to complete each sentence.

EXAMPLE: (**Who,** Whom)   is coming to visit?

5.   Is this the man   (who, whom)   you saw at the game?

6.   This is the woman   (who, that)   is replacing Marlene.

7.   Cats are the animals   (who, that)   I like best.

8.   (Who, Whom)   did Marvin say would take the job?

Part C.   Underline the correct pronouns to complete each sentence.

EXAMPLE: (Them, **Those**)   are my books.

9.   They   (themselves, theirselves)   admitted it was a mistake.

10.   (Those there, Those)   are my best drawings.

11.   I love   (this kind, these kind, these kinds)   of shop.

12.   They sent entry forms to   (myself, me)   and one other person.

Part D.   Underline the correct words to complete each sentence.

EXAMPLE: (**Whose,** Who's)   coat is this in   (**their,** they're)   closet?

13.   This soft drink has lost   (it's, its)   fizz.

14.   Does everyone have   (his or her, their, they're)   assignment?

15.   Your apartment is twice the size of   (ours, our's).

16.   The employees collect   (their, they're)   paychecks on Friday.

Part E.   Underline the correct pronoun to complete each sentence.

EXAMPLE: One of the boys injured   (**his,** their)   arm during the game.

17.   Either Norman or Terry will bring   (his, their)   guitar.

18. Francine, along with her friends, must have thanked   (her, their)   lucky stars.

19. The staff will turn in   (their, its)   report by Friday.

20. No one will get in without   (her or his, their)   ticket.

Skills Correlation Chart for Pretest

After you check your answers, look at the following chart. Circle the number of each question you missed. Then study the subskill in which the skills for the questions you missed are explained.

		QUESTION NUMBER	SUBSKILL NUMBER	SUBSKILL NAME	PAGE NUMBER
Skill Unit One	RECOGNIZING AND CAPITALIZING NOUNS	1 2 3 4	1A	Identifying Nouns	pages 24–26
		5 6 7 8	1B	Identifying Proper Nouns and Common Nouns	pages 26–30
		9 10 11 12	1C	Recognizing Noun Determiners	pages 30–32
		13 14 15 16	1D	Recognizing Noun Endings	pages 32–33
		17 18 19 20	1E	Other Capitalization Rules	pages 33–40
		If you correctly answered 15 or fewer questions, you should study the subskills in Unit One for the questions you missed. If you correctly answered 16 or more of the questions in Unit One, go to Skill Unit Two.			
Skill Unit Two	USING THE PLURAL AND POSSESSIVE FORMS OF NOUNS	1 2 3 4 5 6	2A	Writing the Plural Forms of Nouns	pages 44–47
		7 8 9 10 11	2B	Writing the Possessive Forms of Nouns	pages 47–50
		12 13 14 15 16	2C	Recognizing Noun Forms	pages 50–53
		17 18 19 20	2D	Choosing the Correct Noun Form	pages 53–56
		If you correctly answered 15 or fewer questions, you should study the subskills in Unit Two for the questions you missed. If you correctly answered 16 or more of the questions in Unit Two, go to Skill Unit Three.			
Skill Unit Three	REVIEWING VERBS	1 2 3 4	3A	Identifying Sentence Parts	pages 58–62
		5 6 7 8	3B	Recognizing Action Verbs	pages 62–64
		9 10 11 12	3C	Recognizing Verb Phrases	pages 65–68
		13 14 15 16	3D	Recognizing Linking Verbs	pages 68–71
		17 18 19 20	3E	Identifying Linking Verbs and Helping Verbs	pages 71–74
		21 22 23	3F	Identifying Linking Verbs and Action Verbs	pages 74–75
		If you correctly answered 17 or fewer questions, you should study the subskills in Unit Three for the questions you missed. If you correctly answered 18 or more of the questions in Unit Three, go to Skill Unit Four.			

		QUESTION NUMBER	SUBSKILL NUMBER	SUBSKILL NAME	PAGE NUMBER
Skill Unit Four	USING VERB TENSES CORRECTLY	1 2 3	4A	Using Verbs Correctly in the Present Tense	pages 77–81
		4 5 6	4B	Using Verbs Correctly in the Past Tense	pages 81–84
		7 8 9	4C	Using Verbs Correctly in the Future Tense	pages 84–87
		10 11 12	4D	Using Past Participles to Form the Perfect Tenses	pages 88–92
			If you correctly answered 9 or fewer questions, you should study the subskills in Unit Four for the questions you missed. If you correctly answered 10 or more of the questions in Unit Four, go to Skill Unit Five.	
Skill Unit Five	USING PROGRESSIVE FORMS AND IRREGULAR VERBS	1 2 3 4 5	5A	Using the Progressive Forms of Tenses Correctly	pages 95–101
		6 7 8 9 10	5B	Using the Past and Past Participle Forms of Irregular Verbs Correctly	pages 101–107
		11 12 13	5C	Using Some Problem Verbs Correctly	pages 107–113
			If you correctly answered 9 or fewer questions, you should study the subskills in Unit Five for the questions you missed. If you correctly answered 10 or more of the questions in Unit Five, go to Skill Unit Six.	
Skill Unit Six	IDENTIFYING ADJECTIVES AND USING THEM CORRECTLY	1 2 3 4 5	6A	Identifying Adjectives	pages 114–123
		6 7 8 9 10	6B	Locating Adjectives by Their Position in the Sentence	pages 124–128
		11 12 13 14 15	6C	Recognizing Adjectives by Their Endings	pages 128–131
		16 17 18 19 20	6D	Using Adjectives to Make Comparisons	pages 131–136
			If you correctly answered 15 or fewer questions, you should study the subskills in Unit Six for the questions you missed. If you correctly answered 16 or more of the questions in Unit Six, go to Skill Unit Seven.	
Skill Unit Seven	IDENTIFYING ADVERBS AND USING THEM CORRECTLY	1 2 3 4	7A	Identifying Adverbs	pages 138–143
		5 6 7 8	7B	Positioning Adverbs in a Sentence	pages 143–145
		9 10 11	7C	Forming Adverbs From Adjectives	pages 145–149
		12 13 14	7D	Using Adverbs to Make Comparisons	pages 149–152
		15 16 17	7E	Choosing Between Adjectives and Adverbs	pages 152–155
		18 19 20	7F	Usage Problems With Certain Adverbs	pages 155–158
			If you correctly answered 15 or fewer questions, you should study the subskills in Unit Seven for the questions you missed. If you correctly answered 16 or more of the questions in Unit Seven, go to Skill Unit Eight.	
Skill Unit Eight	USING PREPOSITIONAL PHRASES AS MODIFIERS	1 2 3 4 5 6 7 8	8A	Identifying Prepositional Phrases	pages 161–165
		9 10 11 12 13 14 15 16 17 18 19 20	8B	Using Prepositional Phrases Effectively	pages 165–169
			If you correctly answered 15 or fewer questions, you should study the subskills in Unit Eight for the questions you missed. If you correctly answered 16 or more of the questions in Unit Eight, go to Skill Unit Nine.	

		QUESTION NUMBER	SUBSKILL NUMBER	SUBSKILL NAME	PAGE NUMBER
Skill Unit Nine	SIMPLE SENTENCE PATTERNS	1 2 3 4 5 6	9A	Identifying Action Verb Sentence Patterns	pages 173–180
		7 8 9 10 11 12 13 14	9B	Identifying Linking Verb Sentence Patterns	pages 180–184
		15 16 17 18 19 20	9C	Identifying the Sentence Parts of Special Sentences	pages 184–188
		If you correctly answered 15 or fewer questions, you should study the subskills in Unit Nine for the questions you missed. If you correctly answered 16 or more of the questions in Unit Nine, go to Skill Unit Ten.			
Skill Unit Ten	USING PRONOUNS CORRECTLY	1 2 3 4	10A	Using Subject and Object Pronouns Correctly	pages 191–199
		5 6 7 8	10B	Using Interrogative and Relative Pronouns Correctly	pages 199–205
		9 10 11 12	10C	Using Demonstrative and Reflexive/Intensive Pronouns Correctly	pages 205–209
		13 14 15 16	10D	Using Possessive Pronouns, Their Contraction Sound-Alikes, and Indefinite Pronouns Correctly	pages 209–215
		17 18 19 20	10E	Making Pronouns Agree With Their Antecedents	pages 216–220
		If you correctly answered 15 or fewer questions, you should study the subskills in Unit Ten for the questions you missed. If you correctly answered 16 or more of the questions in Unit Ten, go to Book Three.			

Skill Unit 1
RECOGNIZING AND CAPITALIZING NOUNS

What Skills You Need to Begin: None.

What Skills You Will Learn: After studying this skill unit, you will be able to identify nouns. You will identify common nouns and proper nouns. You will be able to capitalize proper nouns and be able to apply other rules of capitalization. You will also recognize noun determiners and special noun endings.

Why You Need These Skills: By far the largest group of words in our language is made up of nouns—words that name someone or something. In fact, a language that did not allow people to talk about things, places, or people would be of little or no use. Children learning to speak begin by saying such words as <u>daddy</u>, <u>mommy</u>, and <u>doggie</u>. These beginning vocabulary words are nouns. Without even knowing it, children start by learning a most important part of the English language. Since nouns do a lot of the work when we speak and write, it is important to be able to recognize them and understand the different ways in which they are used.

The rules of capitalization are also very important. The most important rule requires each new sentence to begin with a capital letter, to separate one complete idea from another. Capitalization rules are based on a general agreement among the users of the English language. When you follow these rules, you are said to be following the "conventions" of the written language. As English developed, its users agreed, for example, to capitalize proper nouns, such as <u>Tom Jones</u> and <u>New York</u>, but not to capitalize common nouns, such as <u>apple</u> and <u>book</u>.

How You Will Show What You Have Learned: You will take the Self-Check at the end of this unit on page 41. The Self-Check consists of two parts. In the first part, you will be asked to identify the nouns in 10 sentences containing 30 nouns. In the second part, you will be asked to capitalize words in 10 sentences. If you correctly answer 16 of 20 items, you will have shown that you have mastered these skills.

If you feel that you have already mastered these skills, turn to the end of this unit and complete the Self-Check on page 41.

Subskill 1A: Identifying Nouns

When you complete this subskill, you will be able to identify nouns and tell whether each noun names a person, a place, or a thing.

Nouns

The word <u>noun</u> means <u>name</u>. Why, then, do we complicate matters by using <u>noun</u> instead of just saying <u>name</u>? The reason is that we need a term that will mean somewhat more than the word <u>name</u> as we usually use it.

For example, the words <u>Tom</u>, <u>Dick</u> and <u>Harry</u> are names. Anyone can recognize that they are. They are also nouns. But the word <u>noun</u> also includes other kinds of names. Some nouns name things people can see, touch, taste, or smell. <u>Desk</u>, <u>glass</u>, <u>hotel</u>, <u>pie</u>, and <u>rose</u> are all nouns. Other nouns name feelings, qualities or ideas. The words <u>gentleness</u>, <u>truth</u>, and <u>resentment</u> are all nouns.

Perhaps you have learned before that **a noun is the name of a person, place, or thing.** That definition will serve as long as you remember that nouns include some "things" that you can't see, hear, touch, taste, or smell.

Study the following list of the kinds of things nouns can name:

NAMES OF PERSONS: man, soldier, Betty, Jim

NAMES OF PLACES: South America, Rocky Mountains, city, country

NAMES OF CONCRETE OBJECTS: house, ax, paper, bricks

NAMES OF ANIMALS: dog, tiger, ox

NAMES OF ASPECTS OF NATURE: sky, wave, mountain

NAMES OF SUBSTANCES: iron, wood, earth, air, water, steel

NAMES OF STUDIES: arithmetic, philosophy, grammar, science

NAMES OF PROCESSES: division, removal, registration

NAMES OF PROPERTIES: color, weight, density

NAMES OF QUALITIES: kindness, courage, heroism, generosity, weightlessness

NAMES OF MEASURES: inch, peck, pound, acre, meter

NAMES OF STATES OF MIND: worry, care, joy, concentration, attention, indifference

Remember that many words may be nouns in some circumstances and not in others. The noun must be naming something or someone.

(1) The <u>train</u> will be late.

(2) They train horses to jump.

In sentence 1, the word <u>train</u> is the name of something and is a noun. In sentence 2, the word <u>train</u> does not name something and is not a noun.

(1) She swept the <u>walk</u>.

(2) They walk to work.

In sentence 1, the word <u>walk</u> is the name of something and is a noun. In sentence 2, the word <u>walk</u> is an action, not the name of something.

Apply what you have learned about identifying nouns by completing the following exercise.

Exercise for Subskill 1A

Read the following sentences and underline the nouns used in each sentence. Then write <u>person</u>, <u>place</u>, or <u>thing</u> above each noun to show what it names.

                   person   thing
EXAMPLE: The <u>woman</u> parked the <u>car</u>.

1. The soldier stood at the gate.

2. Charity begins at home.

3. That girl likes music and sports.

4. Math is an interesting subject.

5. The children run fast.

6. My cousin lives in another town.

7. Gold is valuable.

8. The knife was not very sharp.

9. Dogs and cats make good pets.

10. The weather changed suddenly.

Check your answers on page 8 in the Answer Key for Book Two. If you correctly identified the nouns and what they name in all 10 sentences, go on to Subskill 1B. If not, complete the Supplemental Exercise for Subskill 1A.

Supplemental Exercise for Subskill 1A

Review the information about nouns on pages 24 and 25. Then complete the following exercise.

Underline each noun in the sentences below.

EXAMPLE: The <u>boy</u> chased his <u>kite</u>.

1. The man listened to every word the woman said.
2. Cincinnati is a city in Ohio.
3. Which artist painted that picture?
4. Janice will visit her friend soon.
5. The new program is not very good.
6. Plant the shrubs near the sidewalk.
7. My sister has a new job.
8. Steel is known for its great strength.
9. Bob has a good imagination.
10. Herds of cattle used to roam the plains.

Check your answers on pages 8 and 9 in the Answer Key for Book Two. If you correctly identified the nouns in 8 of 10 sentences, go to Subskill 1B. If not, ask your instructor for help.

Subskill 1B: Identifying Proper Nouns and Common Nouns

When you complete this subskill, you will be able to identify common nouns and proper nouns. You will capitalize the first letter of all proper nouns.

Proper Nouns

Some nouns name particular persons, places, or things. For example, the noun <u>Steve Marshall</u> is the name of a particular person. The noun <u>Tennessee</u> is the name of a particular place. The noun <u>Academy Award</u> is the name of a particular award. **Nouns that name particular persons, places, or things are called proper nouns.**

Proper nouns always begin with a capital letter. Notice that a proper noun may have more than one word in it. When a proper noun is made up of more than one word, it is still considered one noun.

Usually, all the words in the name begin with a capital letter. For example, the words <u>Mississippi River</u> make one proper noun because together the two words name one particular place. Both words begin with a capital letter.

Common Nouns

Some nouns do not name particular persons, places, or things. For example, the noun <u>man</u> refers to a whole category of persons. It does not tell you the name of a particular person. The noun <u>state</u> does not tell you the name of any particular place. The noun <u>award</u> does not tell you the name of any particular award. The nouns <u>man</u>, <u>state</u>, and <u>award</u> are called **common nouns** because they **are not the names of any particular person, place, or thing.** Common nouns do not begin with a capital letter.

Study the examples in the following chart:

	Common Nouns (name a category)	**Proper Nouns (name a particular person, place, or thing)**
PERSONS	girl boy teacher	Alice Jim Ms. Armstrong
PLACES	city state country river street	Omaha, Los Angeles Nebraska, New Hampshire France, Canada Ohio River Smith Street
THINGS	holiday month day of the week business war organization car school	Thanksgiving February Wednesday Sears, Anderson Plumbing, Time, Inc. World War I National Wildlife Federation Chevrolet, Datsun Hamilton High School, Westvale Community College, University of Pittsburgh

The common nouns name categories of persons, places, and things, while the proper nouns name particular persons, places, and things.

Notice that in proper nouns such as <u>Ohio River</u>, <u>Smith Street</u>, and <u>Westvale Community College</u>, the words <u>river</u>, <u>street</u>, and <u>community college</u> are capitalized along with the specific names.

Notice that for other proper nouns consisting of more than one word, each word is capitalized, except for short prepositions such as <u>of</u>. You will learn more about capitalizing names that consist of more than one word in Subskill 1E.

NOTE: There are two major exceptions to the general rule.

Rule 1:   Do not capitalize the names of the seasons.

summer   spring   winter   fall   autumn

Rule 2:   Do not capitalize school subjects unless they contain a proper noun or a word formed from a proper noun or unless they refer to a particular course name.

I studied history and biology this year.

I am studying <u>F</u>rench and <u>E</u>nglish this year.

I am studying <u>A</u>merican history this year.

I am enrolled in <u>B</u>iology II, <u>A</u>lgebra I, and <u>I</u>ntroduction to <u>L</u>iterature.

Apply what you have learned so far by doing the following exercise.

Exercise for Subskill 1B

Rewrite the sentence in each pair that contains proper nouns and capitalize the proper nouns.

EXAMPLE: **a.**   They are coming on friday.
                 b.   They are coming in two days.

_____They are coming on Friday._____

1. **a.**   Is the bank on the corner of that street?
    b.   Is lincoln savings bank on the corner of chestnut street?

    _____

    _____

2. **a.**   I think that jennifer works for ford motors.
    b.   I think that the woman works for the company.

    _____

    _____

3. **a.**   Will valentine's day be on tuesday this year?
    b.   Will the holiday be on a different day of the week this year?

    _____

    _____

4. a. The mississippi river flows into the gulf of mexico at new orleans.
   b. The river flows into the gulf in this city.

_____

_____

5. a. Is Joe taking the course in chemistry at the college this fall?
   b. Is Joe taking chemistry 101 at smithvale college in september?

_____

_____

Check your answers on page 9 in the Answer Key for Book Two. If you correctly answered all 5 items, go to Subskill 1C. If not, do the Supplemental Exercise for Subskill 1B.

Supplemental Exercise for Subskill 1B

Review the information about common nouns and proper nouns on pages 26–28. Then do the following exercise.

Rewrite the sentence in each pair that contains proper nouns and capitalize the proper nouns.

EXAMPLE: a. I think the man works in the city.
          b. I think george works in chicago.

_____I think George works in Chicago._____

1. a. Did the girl come to see you the other day?
   b. Did sarah come to see you on sunday?

_____

_____

2. a. We know that the holiday is celebrated on the same day every summer.
   b. We know that independence day is celebrated on july 4.

_____

_____

3. a. Is tom going to take american history 101 or economics 201 at jackson high school?
   b. Is your son going to take history or economics at that school?

_____

_____

4. **a.** She said that the man had fought in the war.
    b. She said that jerry simpson had fought in the vietnam war.

    _____

    _____

5. **a.** Has the woman bought a new car?
    b. Has mrs. gomez bought a new pontiac?

    _____

    _____

Check your answers on page 9 in the Answer Key for Book Two. If you correctly answered all 5 items, go to Subskill 1C. If not, ask your instructor for help.

Subskill 1C: Recognizing Noun Determiners

When you complete this subskill, you will be able to recognize noun determiners and use them to help you identify nouns in sentences.

Noun Determiners

There are some words in English that often help us to determine whether or not a given word is a noun. These words are called **noun determiners** or **noun markers.** That is, they "determine" or "mark" that a noun will follow. Some noun determiners are the little words we call **articles** (a, an, and the). Other determiners are words such as the following, which are known as **possessive pronouns:** his, her, your, my, our, and their. Another group of markers is made up of the words this, that, these, those, when they are used to point something out (this hat, that book, these men, those boats). When you see a determiner in a sentence, it will usually be followed by a noun. Often the noun will be the very next word after the determiner.

> The child walked into our yard and fell over a bucket of sand.

In the preceding sentence, a noun comes directly after each determiner. Not all nouns are marked by determiners (as you can see with sand). However, when you see one of the noun determiners, you should look for the noun that will usually follow.

Sometimes the noun is not the very next word after the determiner. There may be words that come between the determiner and the noun. These words usually describe the noun.

> The little child walked into our messy yard and fell over a large bucket of sand.

In this sentence, the determiner <u>the</u> still marks the noun <u>child</u>. The word <u>little</u> is not the noun because it does not name a person, place, or thing. The determiner <u>our</u> still marks the noun <u>yard</u>. The word <u>messy</u> is not a noun because it does not name a person, place, or thing. The determiner <u>a</u> still marks the noun <u>bucket</u>. The word <u>large</u> is not the noun because it does not name a person, place, or thing.

Apply what you have learned about noun determiners by doing the following exercise.

Exercise for Subskill 1C

Carefully read the following sentences. Underline each noun determiner and circle the noun that it is signaling.

EXAMPLE: <u>My</u> (husband) ate <u>the</u> last (cookie) in <u>the</u> (bag).

1. That book should be placed on her desk beside the paper.

2. An old lady walked down the street and hummed a happy song.

3. His car had a flat tire.

4. We went to a party at their new house.

5. Those red flowers are poisonous.

Check your answers on page 9 in the Answer Key for Book Two. If you correctly identified the determiners and the nouns they mark in all 5 sentences, go to Subskill 1D. If not, do the Supplemental Exercise for Subskill 1C.

Supplemental Exercise for Subskill 1C

Review the information about noun determiners on page 30 and on this page. Then do the following exercise.

Carefully read the following sentences. Underline each noun determiner and circle the noun that it signals.

EXAMPLE: <u>His</u> blue (jacket) has <u>a</u> warm (hood).

1. These workers consider the wages too low.

2. Their apartment has two bedrooms.

3. They went on a picnic with her new friends.

4. An excited child spotted the little squirrel.

5. That letter is from my mother.

Check your answers on page 9 in the Answer Key for Book Two. If you correctly identified the determiners and the nouns they mark in 4 of 5 items, go to Subskill 1D. If not, ask your instructor for help.

Subskill 1D: Recognizing Noun Endings

When you complete this subskill, you will be able to identify nouns that have special noun endings.

Noun Endings

Certain **suffixes (word endings)** are often used to form nouns. You can identify some nouns by looking for the following noun endings:

-er:	farmer, worker, partner, carpenter
-or:	actor, doctor, factor
-tion, -sion:	attention, occasion, accumulation
-ment:	department, employment, equipment
-ness:	happiness, goodness, greatness
ance, -ence:	endurance, repentance, independence
-ure:	pleasure, creature, failure
-ity, -iety:	anxiety, reality, creativity

Apply what you have learned about noun endings by doing the following exercise.

Exercise for Subskill 1D

In the following sentences there are 12 nouns that have special noun endings. Underline each noun that has a special noun ending.

EXAMPLE: My employer pays for my health insurance.

1.   The entertainment was provided by a singer and a juggler.

2.   Filling out the application took intelligence and concentration.

3.   It's my pleasure to thank you for your kindness.

4.   His failure caused great anxiety.

5.   It is Jane's responsibility to check the equipment.

Check your answers on page 9 in the Answer Key for Book Two. If you correctly identified all 12 nouns with special noun endings, go to Subskill 1E. If not, do the Supplemental Exercise for Subskill 1D.

Supplemental Exercise for Subskill 1D

Review the information about special noun endings on page 32. Then do the following exercise.

In the following sentences, there are 12 nouns with special noun endings. Underline each noun with a special noun ending.

EXAMPLE: The <u>workers</u> in that <u>department</u> are known for their <u>helpfulness</u>.

1. Runners must have physical endurance and flexibility.

2. Jack's promotion caused great happiness.

3. Their decision was not based on reality.

4. She used a calculator to do the addition and subtraction.

5. Thank you for your assistance and encouragement.

Check your answers on page 10 in the Answer Key for Book Two. If you correctly identified 10 of 12 nouns with special endings, go to Subskill 1E. If not, ask your instructor for help.

Subskill 1E: Other Capitalization Rules

When you complete this subskill, you will be able to apply the rules of capitalization to specific troublesome cases.

Being able to identify proper nouns is the first step to using capital letters correctly. However, you may still be unsure about whether to capitalize certain kinds of words. The following sets of rules should help.

Rules That Apply to People

Rule 1: Capitalize family relationships (<u>mother</u>, <u>father</u>, <u>grandmother</u>, <u>uncle</u>, etc.) only when they are used with a name or in the place of a name.

I believe <u>U</u>ncle Charles left for home this morning.

In this sentence, <u>uncle</u> is capitalized because it is used with the name <u>Charles</u>.

He usually calls <u>M</u>other before he leaves.

<u>Mother</u> is capitalized because it is used in place of someone's real name. The woman's real name may be Mary Alice Blackstone, but her chil-

dren call her <u>M</u>other. You could substitute the woman's real name and the sentence would still make sense.

My <u>m</u>other gets upset when he doesn't call.

<u>Mother</u> is not capitalized in this example because <u>mother</u> is not used as a name. It merely indicates a relationship. The word <u>my</u> is the tip-off here. You can't substitute a person's name after a possessive pronoun. That is, you could not say, "My Mary Alice Blackstone gets upset when he doesn't call."

On my birthday <u>G</u>randmother gave me the usual shirt and tie.

<u>Grandmother</u> is used in the place of someone's name. Her name may be Helen Beth Robinson, but to the writer her name is "Grandmother."

James says his grandmother always sends him money.

The possessive pronoun <u>his</u> is a tip-off that <u>grandmother</u> is not being used in place of someone's real name. It merely indicates a relationship. You could not say, "His Helen Beth Robinson sends him money."

Our <u>A</u>unt Carol is the best cook I know.

Although the possessive pronoun <u>our</u> is used with the relationship, <u>aunt</u> is still capitalized because it is used with the name <u>Carol</u>.

Rule 2:   Capitalize professional and political titles only when they are used with a name or in the place of a name. The exception to this is the word <u>President</u>, which is always capitalized when it refers to the President of the United States.

I call <u>D</u>octor Whitely when I need my prescription refilled.

<u>Doctor</u> is capitalized because it it used with the last name Whitely.

Well, <u>D</u>octor, can you help me?

<u>Doctor</u> is capitalized because it is used in place of the person's name. You could substitute the name <u>Jane</u> or the name <u>John</u>, and the sentence would still make sense.

She is one <u>d</u>octor who doesn't mind being called at home.

<u>Doctor</u> is not capitalized because it is neither used with a name nor in the place of a name. Study the following additional pairs that illustrate this rule:

Allen was a <u>s</u>ergeant.
<u>S</u>ergeant Samuels gave an order.

My <u>p</u>rofessor gave only one test during the entire semester.
Have you met <u>P</u>rofessor Hill?

Preston Smith was <u>g</u>overnor for more than one term.
I once heard <u>G</u>overnor Smith give a moving speech.

Who will be elected <u>s</u>enator?
<u>S</u>enator Dubinsky visited our town.

Remember the following exception:

The <u>P</u>resident welcomed each diplomat with a handshake.

The word <u>President</u> is always capitalized when it refers to the President of the United States.

BUT: The president of the union addressed the convention.

Rule 3:   Capitalize the personal pronoun <u>I</u> and the contractions <u>I</u>'m, <u>I</u>'ll, <u>I</u>'ve, and <u>I</u>'d.

If <u>I</u>'ve finished the job by then, <u>I</u>'ll let you know.

Do you think <u>I</u> need my umbrella today?

Rule 4:   Capitalize a person's initials, since they stand for the person's name.

Have you read any books by <u>H</u>. <u>G</u>. Wells?

Rules That Apply to Places

Rule 1:   Capitalize <u>north</u>, <u>south</u>, <u>east</u>, <u>west</u> when they refer to sections of the United States or sections of the world but not when they are used to indicate a direction. If you can substitute the words <u>right</u> or <u>left</u> for the direction, then do not capitalize it.

Turn <u>s</u>outh on Highway 39.

<u>South</u> is not capitalized because it is used as a direction, like <u>right</u> or <u>left</u>.

The Middle East has been an area of concern for us in recent years.

The <u>Middle East</u> refers to a geographical section of the world. Therefore, it is capitalized.

The new shopping center is <u>w</u>est of Gilmer Street.

The word <u>west</u> is not capitalized because it is used to indicate a direction.

Rule 2:   You know that the names of specific places are capitalized. So are the names of specific languages, the names of nationalities, and the names of the inhabitants of a specific place. Also capitalize words that are formed from such proper nouns.

He went to <u>C</u>hina.   (place)

Does she speak <u>C</u>hinese?   (language)

The <u>C</u>hinese are proud of their ancient civilization.   (inhabitants)

She is <u>C</u>hinese.   (nationality)

We saw a beautiful <u>C</u>hinese vase in the museum.   (word formed from proper noun)

Rules That Apply to Politics and Government

Rule 1: Capitalize the names of a specific political party and the name of a member of that party.

>The symbol of the Republican Party is an elephant.

>She is a registered Democrat.

>Our state is represented by two Democratic senators.

>NOTE: When the word democratic is used to describe a type of government, it is not capitalized.

>>The United States has a democratic government.

Rule 2: Capitalize the names of specific government bodies and organizations.

>We ordered some pamphlets from the Department of Agriculture.

>The Senate and the House of Representatives make the laws we live under. Together, they are known as Congress.

Rule 3: For the titles of people in government, follow the rule you have learned about other titles. If the title is used with the person's name or in place of the person's name, capitalize it. If not, do not capitalize it.

>The senator will speak at the rally.

>Will Senator Ingram be speaking at the rally?

>Tell me, Senator, will you be speaking at the rally?

Rules That Apply to Religion

Rule 1: Capitalize the names of specific religions and the members of those religions.

>Christianity and Judaism are two of the world's major religions.

>Christians and Jews will both celebrate religious holidays this week.

Rule 2: Capitalize the names of sacred figures of a religion.

>>God   Jesus Christ

>>Jehovah   Christ the Lord

>>Allah

NOTE: Do not capitalize the word <u>god</u> when it refers to the gods of mythology. But capitalize the names of individual gods.

Was <u>M</u>ars the Greek god of war?

Rule 3:   Capitalize the names of sacred books.

the <u>B</u>ible

the <u>T</u>orah

the <u>K</u>oran

the <u>N</u>ew <u>T</u>estament

Rules That Apply to Sentences, Quotations, and Letters

Rule 1:   Capitalize the first word in a sentence.

<u>H</u>e just learned to drive.

<u>T</u>ake your time.

<u>W</u>here is Bob?

Rule 2:   Capitalize the first word in a direct quotation. A direct quotation tells the exact words someone says. It is set off by quotation marks.

Sue said, "<u>S</u>ometimes this room gets too warm."

NOTE: When a one-sentence quotation is split up, only the first part of the quotation begins with a capital letter.

"<u>S</u>ometimes," Sue said, "this room gets too warm."

If the second part of a split quotation begins a new sentence, then both parts of the quotation begin with a capital letter.

"<u>S</u>ometimes this room gets too warm," Sue said. "<u>T</u>hen I have to turn down the thermostat."

Rule 3:   Capitalize the first word in the greeting of a letter. Also capitalize any names or words that stand in for names.

<u>D</u>ear Angela,

<u>D</u>ear Aunt Sally,

<u>D</u>ear Ms. Forrester,

<u>D</u>ear Mother,

<u>D</u>ear Mr. Schultz,

Rule 4: Capitalize the first word in the closing of a letter. Do not capitalize any other words in the closing.

Sincerely,

Yours truly,

Very truly yours,

Your friend,

Apply what you have learned about capitalization by doing the following exercise.

Exercise for Subskill 1E

Rewrite the sentences below, capitalizing all words that need to be capitalized.

EXAMPLE: my favorite chinese restaurant is west of the new hospital.

My favorite Chinese restaurant is west of the new hospital.

1. years ago, grandmother saw the opening of the panama canal.

   _____

   _____

2. last spring we moved from a small town in the south to a large city in the north.

   _____

   _____

3. yours very truly, j.t. gray
   (Capitalize as in the closing of a letter.)

   _____

4. after this semester i'll need one credit in english, two in american history, and three in math.

   _____

   _____

5. "please have a seat," the secretary requested, "and i will tell the doctor you're here."

   _____

   _____

6. a republican from our state was just elected to the united states senate.

_____

_____

7. there is a baptist church two blocks north of here.

_____

8. i have several chinese vases that my uncle sent from the far east.

_____

_____

9. in may, the visiting general inspected the troops and reported to congress.

_____

_____

10. dear ms. randolph,   (Capitalize as in the greeting of a letter.)

_____

Check your answers on page 10 in the Answer Key for Book Two. If you correctly answered all 10 items, go to the Self-Check. If not, do the Supplemental Exercise for Subskill 1E.

Supplemental Exercise for Subskill 1E

Review the capitalization rules on pages 33–38. Then do the following exercise.

Rewrite the sentences on the next page, capitalizing all words that need to be capitalized.

EXAMPLE: the minister of national defense made a speech to the house of commons yesterday.

The Minister of National Defense made a speech to the House of Commons yesterday.

1. two senators from the democratic party met with the president yesterday.

_____

_____

2. my uncle charlie likes books about the old west.

_____

3. "tell us, senator," the reporter said, "what you plan to do."

_____

4. that novel was written by the american author ernest hemingway.

_____

_____

5. dear aunt ruth,
   (Capitalize as in the greeting of a letter.)

_____

6. when it got dark, i turned west, took the road into town, and found a good italian restaurant.

_____

_____

7. "to everything there is a season," the bible says, "and a time to every purpose under the heaven."

_____

_____

8. the speaker at the banquet was doctor j.t. jones.

_____

_____

9. did you visit a buddhist temple while you were in the far east?

_____

_____

10. she is studying english, typing, and stenography.

_____

Check your answers on page 10 in the Answer Key for Book Two. If you correctly answered 8 of 10 items, go to the Self-Check. If not, ask your instructor for help.

SELF-CHECK: SKILL UNIT 1

Part A. Circle all the nouns in the following sentences. You should find 30 nouns in all. Use your knowledge of noun determiners and special noun endings to help you.

EXAMPLE: Their (vacation) was spent at (Sunrise Lake).

1. A small kitten lay sleeping on the rug beside the fire.

2. His failure caused great sadness.

3. Our decision will depend largely on your suggestion.

4. Thomas Edison was a great man and an ingenious inventor.

5. Several girls rode their bicycles on Main Street.

6. The Pacific Ocean lies off the coast of California.

7. Loyalty, honor, truthfulness, and love are all important qualities.

8. Imagination is a necessity for a growing mind.

9. The Russians and the Americans reached an agreement.

10. The flock of geese flew over our heads.

Part B. Rewrite the following sentences, capitalizing all words that should be capitalized according to standard rules of capitalization.

EXAMPLE: today is wednesday, july 7, so he must be in pittsburgh.

   Today is Wednesday, July 7, so he must be in Pittsburgh.

11. last summer i took science 101 at southwestern university.

_____

_____

12. "are you going to aunt milly's with us at christmas," father asked, "or will you be out of town?"

_____

_____

13. we visited the golden gate bridge when we went to california last summer.

_____

_____

14. on wednesday the class heard senator smith address the united states congress.

_____

_____

15. yours respectfully,   (Capitalize as in the
    john steinberg   closing of a letter.)

_____

_____

16. the west is still more thinly populated than other sections of the united states.

_____

_____

17. the city is planning to connect mockingbird lane with the new highway.

_____

_____

18. the minister and the congregation prayed to god.

_____

_____

19. i love dutch chocolates, italian ices, and french vanilla ice cream.

_____

_____

20. drive east for two miles until you get to webster avenue.

_____

_____

Check your answers on pages 10 and 11 in the Answer Key for Book Two. If you correctly answered 16 of 20 items, you have shown that you have mastered these skills. If not, ask your instructor for help.

Skill Unit 2
USING THE PLURAL AND POSSESSIVE FORMS OF NOUNS

What Skills You Need to Begin: You need to be able to identify nouns.

What Skills You Will Learn: After completing this skill unit, you will be able to write the plural forms, the singular possessive form, and the plural possessive form of nouns. You will be able to identify each form and tell when it is needed.

Why You Need These Skills: Most nouns can be written in four different forms. One form of the noun is used to talk about one person, place, or thing. Another form is used to talk about more than one person, place, or thing. A third form of the noun is used to show that something belongs to one person, place, or thing. Yet another form shows that something belongs to more than one person, place, or thing. In order to write exactly what you mean to communicate about a noun, you need to recognize these four noun forms and use them correctly.

How You Will Show What You Have Learned: You will take the Self-Check at the end of this unit on page 56. The Self-Check contains 15 sentences. In each sentence you must write correctly the noun form that is needed. If you can write at least 12 of 15 nouns correctly, you will have shown that you have mastered these skills.

If you feel that you have already mastered these skills, turn to the end of this unit and complete the Self-Check on page 56.

Subskill 2A: Writing the Plural Forms of Nouns

When you complete this subskill, you will be able to write the plural forms of nouns.

Singular and Plural

Most nouns have a **singular** form and a **plural** form. The singular form is used to name one person, place, or thing (student, home, bat). The plural form is used to name more than one person, place, or thing (students, homes, bats).

Not all nouns form the plural in the same way. The following rules will help you learn the various ways to make nouns plural.

Forming Plurals

Rule 1:   To form the plural of most nouns, just add s to the singular.

SINGULAR: toy   battle   handful   implication

PLURAL: toys   battles   handfuls   implications

Rule 2:   To form the plural of a noun ending in s, ch, sh, x, or z, add es.

SINGULAR: church   bush   gas   tax   quartz

PLURAL: churches   bushes   gases   taxes   quartzes

Rule 3:   To form the plural of a noun ending in a consonant + y, change the y to i and add es.

SINGULAR: lady   penny   city   jury

PLURAL: ladies   pennies   cities   juries

Rule 4:   To form the plural of a noun ending in a vowel + y, add s.

SINGULAR: monkey   tray   display

PLURAL: monkeys   trays   displays

Rule 5:   To form the plural of a noun ending in a vowel + o, add s.

SINGULAR: rodeo   radio   igloo

PLURAL: rodeos   radios   igloos

Rule 6:   When a word ends in a consonant + o, you may need to check your dictionary to be sure of the correct plural form. For some words ending in a consonant + <u>o</u>, you add <u>s</u> to form the plural. For others, you add <u>es</u>. There are even words that can take either <u>s</u> or <u>es</u>. Memorize the spellings of the following words. Notice that many of the words that just add <u>s</u> have something to do with music.

For the following words, the plural is formed by adding <u>es</u>:

SINGULAR: potato   tomato   echo   tornado   hero

PLURAL: potato<u>es</u> tomato<u>es</u> echo<u>es</u> tornado<u>es</u> hero<u>es</u>

For the following words, the plural is formed by adding <u>s</u>:

SINGULAR: alto   soprano   piano   banjo   dynamo

PLURAL: alto<u>s</u> soprano<u>s</u> piano<u>s</u> banjo<u>s</u> dynamo<u>s</u>

For some words, like the following, the plural may be formed by adding either <u>s</u> or <u>es</u>:

SINGULAR: zero   mosquito

PLURAL: zero<u>s</u> or zero<u>es</u>   mosquito<u>s</u> or mosquito<u>es</u>

Rule 7: To form the plural of most nouns ending in <u>f</u> or <u>fe</u>, add <u>s</u>.

SINGULAR: belief   roof   chief   handkerchief   safe

PLURAL: belief<u>s</u> roof<u>s</u> chief<u>s</u> handkerchief<u>s</u> safe<u>s</u>

There are twelve common words ending in <u>f</u> or <u>fe</u> that form the plural in a special way. For these words, you must change the <u>f</u> or <u>fe</u> to <u>v</u> and add <u>es</u>. Memorize the spelling of the twelve words.

SINGULAR: half   calf   elf   self   shelf   wolf

PLURAL: hal<u>ves</u> cal<u>ves</u> el<u>ves</u> sel<u>ves</u> shel<u>ves</u> wol<u>ves</u>

SINGULAR: thief   leaf   loaf   life   wife   knife

PLURAL: thie<u>ves</u> lea<u>ves</u> loa<u>ves</u> li<u>ves</u> wi<u>ves</u> kni<u>ves</u>

Rule 8: A few words have special plural forms that have nothing to do with adding <u>s</u> or <u>es</u>. Memorize the spellings of these plurals.

SINGULAR: man woman child   mouse foot tooth goose

PLURAL: men women children mice   feet teeth geese

Rule 9: The plural form of a few nouns is the same as the singular. Some of the most common nouns of this type are listed below.

SINGULAR AND PLURAL: pants   slacks   athletics   politics

scissors   sheep   deer   fish

Apply what you have learned about forming plurals by doing the following exercise.

Exercise for Subskill 2A

Write the plural form of each noun.

EXAMPLE: leaf   _____leaves_____

1. battery   _____
2. tray   _____
3. coach   _____
4. man   _____
5. shelf   _____
6. tooth   _____
7. piano   _____
8. sheep   _____
9. belief   _____
10. tax   _____
11. woman   _____
12. display   _____
13. list   _____
14. hero   _____
15. wife   _____

Check your answers on page 11 in the Answer Key for Book Two. If you correctly wrote all 15 plurals, go to Subskill 2B. If not, do the Supplemental Exercise for Subskill 2A.

Supplemental Exercise for Subskill 2A

Review the information about forming plurals on pages 44 and 45. Then do the following exercise.

Write the plural form of each noun.

EXAMPLE: dream   _____dreams_____

1. monkey   _____
2. cargo   _____

3. message   _____

4. sketch   _____

5. baby   _____

6. house   _____

7. chief   _____

8. potato   _____

9. display   _____

10. radio   _____

11. mouse   _____

12. thief   _____

13. soprano   _____

14. wolf   _____

15. foot   _____

Check your answers on page 11 in the Answer Key for Book Two. If you correctly spelled 12 of 15 plurals, go to Subskill 2B. If not, ask your instructor for help.

Subskill 2B: Writing the Possessive Forms of Nouns

When you complete this subskill, you will be able to write the singular possessive and plural possessive forms of nouns.

Possessive Forms of Nouns

The possessive form of a noun is used to show that something belongs to that person, place, or thing. For example, to show that something belongs to a <u>girl</u>, you would use the possessive form <u>girl's</u>. The apostrophe (') means "of."

> The <u>girl's</u> name is Sarah.
> (The name of the girl is Sarah.)

> The <u>girl's</u> watch was broken.
> (The watch of the girl was broken.)

The following rules tell how to write the possessive forms of nouns:

Rule 1: To write the possessive form of any singular noun, add an apostrophe (') and s to the noun.

man + 's = man's	The man's name is Peter.
Charles + 's = Charles's	Charles's check was missing.
cat + 's = cat's	The cat's tail was white.
boss + 's = boss's	The boss's desk was messy.
child + 's = child's	The child's toy is on the couch.

Note that although Charles and boss end in s, they still follow this rule: Always form the possessive of a singular noun by adding 's.

Rule 2: To write the possessive form of a plural noun that ends in s, just add an apostrophe to the plural form.

cats + ' = cats'	The cats' owner wanted to give them away. (more than one cat)
bosses + ' = bosses'	The bosses' secretaries took turns answering the phones. (more than one boss)

Rule 3: To write the possessive form of a plural noun that does not end in s, add an apostrophe and s to the plural form.

men + 's = men's	The men's names were George and Harry. (more than one man)
children + 's = children's	The children's parents were invited to the program. (more than one child)

Apply what you have learned about forming possessive nouns by doing the following exercise.

Exercise for Subskill 2B

Part A.   Fill in the blanks with the singular possessive form of each noun.

EXAMPLE: girl   the _____girl's_____ picture

1.   child   the _____ mother

2.   man   the _____ car

3.   Mr. Jones   _____ house

4. car	the	_____	engine
5. soldier	the	_____	uniform
6. knife	the	_____	edge
7. woman	the	_____	name
8. sister	the	_____	husband
9. mouse	the	_____	whiskers
10. wife	my	_____	parents

Part B.   Fill in the blanks with the plural possessive form of each noun.

EXAMPLE: girls   the   _____girls'_____   picture

11. children	the	_____	mother
12. men	the	_____	car
13. Joneses	the	_____	house
14. cars	the	_____	engines
15. soldiers	the	_____	brigade
16. knives	the	_____	edges
17. women	the	_____	names
18. sisters	the	_____	husbands
19. mice	the	_____	whiskers
20. wives	the	_____	discussion

Check your answers on page 11 in the Answer Key for Book Two. If you correctly wrote all 20 possessive forms, go to Subskill 2C. If not, do the Supplemental Exercise for Subskill 2B.

Supplemental Exercise for Subskill 2B

Review the information about possessives on pages 47 and 48. Then do the following exercise.

Part A.   Fill in the blanks with the singular possessive form of each noun.

EXAMPLE: boy   the_____boy's_____   shoes

1. baby	the	_____	stroller
2. goose	the	_____	feathers
3. tree	the	_____	branches

4. Lois   _____ job

5. dog   the _____ collar

6. friend   my   _____ mother

7. mouse   the _____ tail

8. James   _____ motorcycle

9. attorney the _____ briefcase

10. child   the _____ toy

Part B. Fill in the blanks with the correct plural possessive form of each noun.

EXAMPLE: students   the___students'___ books

11. babies   the _____ strollers

12. geese   the _____ feathers

13. girls   the _____ bathing suits

14. children the _____ toys

15. five cents   _____ worth

16. witnesses the _____ statements

17. sopranos the _____ voices

18. wolves   the _____ howls

19. bosses   the _____ secretaries

20. women   the _____ jobs

Check your answers on pages 11 and 12 in the Answer Key for Book Two. If you correctly answered 16 of 20 items, go to Subskill 2C. If not, ask your instructor for help.

Subskill 2C: Recognizing Noun Forms

When you complete this subskill, you will be able to recognize the four noun forms: singular, plural, singular possessive, and plural possessive.

Review of Noun Forms

In Subskills 2A and 2B, you learned the four forms a noun can take: singular, plural, singular possessive, and plural possessive.

Notice how the form of the noun <u>girl</u> changes as its meaning changes:

SINGULAR: <u>girl</u> (meaning one girl)
The <u>girl</u> answered my question.

PLURAL: <u>girls</u> (meaning more than one girl)
The <u>girls</u> were playing outside.

SINGULAR
POSSESSIVE: <u>girl's</u> (meaning that something belongs to one girl)
The <u>girl's</u> parents are proud of her.
(The parents <u>of</u> the girl)

PLURAL
POSSESSIVE: <u>girls'</u> (meaning that something belongs to more than one girl)
The <u>girls'</u> parents are proud of them.
(The parents <u>of</u> the girls)

Now notice how the form of the noun <u>woman</u> changes as its meaning changes:

SINGULAR: <u>woman</u> (meaning one woman)
The <u>woman</u> told me to call her tomorrow.

PLURAL: <u>women</u> (meaning more than one woman)
Ten <u>women</u> applied for the job.

SINGULAR
POSSESSIVE: <u>woman's</u> (meaning that something belongs to one woman)
That <u>woman's</u> opinions were interesting.
(The opinion <u>of</u> that woman)

PLURAL
POSSESSIVE: <u>women's</u> (meaning that something belongs to more than one woman)
Those <u>women's</u> opinions were interesting.
(The opinions <u>of</u> those women)

Apply what you have learned about recognizing noun forms by doing the following exercise.

Exercise for Subskill 2C

The chart on page 52 is divided into four columns: Singular, Singular Possessive, Plural, and Plural Possessive. Read the sentences that follow. Underline the nouns in each sentence. Then decide the form of each noun and write the noun in the appropriate column in the chart.

EXAMPLE: <u>Helen's</u> <u>job</u> is important.

	Singular	Singular Possessive	Plural	Plural Possessive
EXAMPLE:	job	Helen's		
1.				
2.				
3.				
4.				
5.				
6.				
7.				
8.				

1.   The members' votes were counted.

2.   Women's dresses are found on two floors of the store.

3.   The child's favorite meal was spaghetti.

4.   The men's coats were hanging near the door.

5.   Chris's gloves are on the table.

6.   James admires the beauty of the scene.

7.   Mr. Jones's walks were covered with snow.

8.   Ross, the watchman, works late at night.

Check your answers on page 12 in the Answer Key for Book Two. If you correctly identified the noun forms in all 8 sentences, go to Subskill 2D. If not, do the Supplemental Exercise for Subskill 2C.

Supplemental Exercise for Subskill 2C

Review the information about the four noun forms on pages 50 and 51. Then do the following exercise.

The chart on page 53 is divided into four columns: Singular, Singular Possessive, Plural, and Plural Possessive. Read the sentences that follow. Underline the nouns in each sentence. Then decide the form of each noun and write the noun in the appropriate column in the chart.

EXAMPLE: The <u>thief</u> took <u>Janet's</u> <u>purse</u>.

	Singular	Singular Possessive	Plural	Plural Possessive
EXAMPLE:	thief purse	Janet's		
1.				
2.				
3.				
4.				
5.				
6.				
7.				
8.				

1. Louis's brothers took a trip to California.

2. The sisters' husbands get along well.

3. Men's shoes were on sale.

4. A child's toys were scattered around the room.

5. Please don't forget to bring matches.

6. Steve bought two loaves of bread.

7. The children's parents attended a meeting.

8. Our neighbor's dogs began to bark.

Check your answers on page 13 in the Answer Key for Book Two. If you correctly identified the noun forms in 6 of 8 sentences, go to Subskill 2D. If not, ask your instructor for help.

Subskill 2D: Choosing the Correct Noun Form

When you complete this subskill, you will be able to use noun forms correctly in sentences.

Deciding Which Form of the Noun You Need

Suppose you have one dog and you want to write a sentence about a collar belonging to that dog. What form of the word <u>dog</u> do you need and how is that form spelled? In other words, how would you fill in the following blank?

My _____ collar is missing.

First, ask yourself how many dogs you are talking about. Since you are talking about only one dog, you will need one of the singular forms of the noun—either the singular or the singular possessive. How do you know which one to choose? Since you are talking about something that belongs to the dog, you will need the singular possessive.

How do you form the possessive form of a singular noun? According to the rules, you should add an apostrophe and <u>s</u> to the singular form. So the word you need in the blank is <u>dog's</u>.

My <u>dog's</u> collar is missing.

You should follow a similar process whenever you are trying to decide which of the four forms of a noun to use. The process can be summarized as follows:

Step 1: Ask yourself whether you are talking about one person, place, or thing, or more than one.

Step 2: If you are talking about one thing, use the singular form. If you are talking about more than one, use the plural form.

Step 3: Now ask yourself whether you are saying that something belongs to the noun. If so, you need a possessive form. If not, leave the noun as is.

Step 4: If you are saying that something belongs to the noun, follow the rules for forming possessives. If the noun is singular, add <u>'s</u>. Add <u>'s</u> even if the singular noun ends in <u>s</u>. If the noun is plural and ends in <u>s</u>, just add an apostrophe. If the noun is plural and does not end in <u>s</u>, add <u>'s</u>.

Apply what you have learned about writing noun forms correctly by doing the following exercise.

Exercise for Subskill 2D

Part A.   Using all the rules you have learned, fill in the blanks with the correct form of the noun needed in each sentence.

EXAMPLE: woman   The _____women's_____ voices blended in harmony.

1. man   The _____ heart had stopped beating.

2. friend   My _____ apartments are all bigger than mine.

3. pilot   Because of the emergency, all of the _____ were put on stand-by.

4. brush   The students were asked to clean their _____ after painting class.

5. James   _____ reasons for quitting his job were not good ones.

Part B.   In each sentence, study the nouns in parentheses. Underline the correct noun form needed in each sentence.

EXAMPLE: The (<u>boys</u>, boy's, boys') left for school on time.

6. Several (parents, parent's, parents') arguments were supported by the School Board.

7. That (witnesses, witness's, witnesses') story was not convincing.

8. The (teachers, teacher's, teachers') had a meeting yesterday.

9. The (boys, boy's, boys') appetite has not been good lately.

10. The (childrens, children's, childrens') lessons were done.

Check your answers on page 13 in the Answer Key for Book Two. If you correctly answered all 10 items, go to the Self-Check on page 56. If not, do the Supplemental Exercise for Subskill 2D.

Supplemental Exercise for Subskill 2D

Review the information on page 54 about choosing the correct noun form. Then do the following exercise.

Part A.   Fill in the blanks with the correct form of the noun needed in each sentence.

1. tornado   A _____ path is marked by death and destruction.

2. coach   The two _____ strategies were similar.

3. tooth   Baby John has a new _____.

4. glass   Joe broke four _____ at the party.

5. story   The _____ ending was sad.

Part B. Underline the correct noun form needed in each sentence.

6. (Wilburs, Wilbur's, Wilburs') bad checks are ruining his credit rating.

7. Those (shelves, shelf's, shelves') should be stronger.

8. The (wives, wife's, wives') opinions were not the same as their husbands'.

9. Betty (Joneses, Jones's, Joneses') car is not the same color as mine.

10. That (watches, watch's, watches') hands are painted with a luminous material.

Check your answers on pages 13 and 14 in the Answer Key for Book Two. If you correctly answered 8 of 10 items, go to the Self-Check. If not, ask your instructor for help.

SELF–CHECK: SKILL UNIT 2

Write the form of the noun that correctly completes each sentence.

EXAMPLE: Ralph   ____Ralph's____ legs are tired.

1. van   The _____ right front tire needs air.

2. party   Al went to three _____ last week.

3. Charles _____ friends were very encouraging.

4. witness How many _____ were there at the scene of the crime?

5. tomato   I bought some fresh _____ .

6. thief   The _____ sentence was one year in jail.

7. calf   The _____ mothers were nearby.

8. piano   The _____ keyboard was made of ivory.

9. life   We will remember this moment all our _____ .

10. Weiss   The _____ relatives are visiting them.

11. mouse   The cat caught three _____ .

12. man   That _____ name is Albert Preston.

13. church   That _____ services are well at-
               tended.

14. woman   The three _____ are old friends.

15. knife   The _____ handles were all made of
               wood.

Check your answers on page 14 of the Answer Key for Book Two. If you wrote 12 of 15 noun forms correctly, you have shown that you have mastered these skills. If not, ask your instructor for help.

Skill Unit 3
REVIEWING VERBS

What Skills You Need to Begin: You need to be able to identify nouns (Skill Unit 1).

What Skills You Will Learn: After completing this skill unit, you will be able to identify the complete subject, the complete predicate, the simple subject, and the verb of a sentence. You will be able to identify action verbs and linking verbs. If the verb consists of more than one word, you will be able to identify the main verb and the helping verbs in the verb phrase.

Why You Need These Skills: The verb in a sentence is like the engine in a car. It is absolutely essential. It gives the sentence its power and movement. Verbs can do different kinds of work in a sentence. You have been using language, especially verbs, almost all of your life. Verbs have been of good service to you, but they can be of better service if you understand how they work. By understanding how verbs function in sentences, you can use verbs more effectively in the sentences you write.

How You Will Show What You Have Learned: You will take the Self-Check at the end of this lesson on page 76. The Self-Check contains 20 sentences. If you correctly identify the verbs in 16 of 20 sentences, you will have shown that you have mastered these skills.

If you feel that you have already mastered these skills, turn to the end of this unit and complete the Self-Check on page 76.

Subskill 3A: Identifying Sentence Parts

When you complete this subskill, you will be able to divide a sentence into two parts: the **complete subject** and the **complete predicate**. You will also be able to identify the simple subject and the simple predicate (verb).

Complete Subject and Complete Predicate

A **sentence** is a group of words that expresses a complete thought. A sentence can be divided into parts: the complete subject and the complete predicate. The **complete subject is made up of all the words that tell who or what is doing the action or being spoken about. The complete predicate is made up of all the words that tell what the subject does or did or what the subject is or was.**

In the following examples, the complete subject of each sentence is to the left of the slash, and the complete predicate is to the right of the slash:

The little spotted dog / ran down the street.

My fragile canoe / floated into the rapids.

That old movie / is my favorite.

The Simple Subject

Notice that each of the complete subjects in the sentences above contains a noun plus words that describe the noun. **The noun in the complete subject that names who or what the sentence is about is called the simple subject.** The simple subjects are labeled S in each of the following sentences.

$$\overset{S}{\text{The little spotted dog}} \quad / \quad \text{ran down the street.}$$

$$\overset{S}{\text{My fragile canoe}} \quad / \quad \text{floated down the rapids.}$$

$$\overset{S}{\text{That old movie}} \quad / \quad \text{is my favorite.}$$

Sometimes the simple subject is not a noun. Sometimes the simple subject is a **pronoun, which is a word that is used to take the place of a noun.** You will learn more about pronouns in Skill Unit 9. For now, you simply need to recognize the pronouns that are often used as simple subjects. These include: I, you, he, she, it, we, they, someone, everyone, each, all, and some. Look at the sentences below to see how a pronoun can take the place of a noun.

(1) Mary / is walking down the hall.

(2) She / is walking down the hall.

In sentence 2, she is a pronoun that takes the place of the noun subject Mary in sentence 1.

(1) Dogs / make good pets.

(2) They / make good pets.

In sentence 2, they is a pronoun that takes the place of the noun subject dogs in sentence 1.

Notice that in each of the four sentences above, there was only one word in the subject. When there is only one noun or pronoun in the subject, that word is the complete subject as well as the simple subject.

The Simple Predicate (Verb)

The complete predicate always includes a verb. **A verb is a word that expresses action or state of being.** Sometimes the verb is called the simple predicate. It is often the easiest part of the sentence to find. The verb is labeled V in each of the following sentences.

$$\begin{array}{ccc} & S & V \\ \text{The little spotted dog} & / & \text{ran down the street.} \end{array}$$

$$\begin{array}{ccc} & S & V \\ \text{My fragile canoe} & / & \text{floated into the rapids.} \end{array}$$

$$\begin{array}{ccc} & S & V \\ \text{That old movie} & / & \text{is my favorite.} \end{array}$$

Now look at some more sentences. The following sentences have been divided into their two main parts: complete subject and complete predicate. The simple subject has been labeled S. The verb has been labeled V. In the first four sentences, the verb expresses action. In the next four sentences, the verb expresses a state of being, which is expressed by forms of the word be, such as am, is, was, are, will be, etc.

$$\begin{array}{ccc} S & & V \\ \text{We} & / & \text{go there on Saturdays.} \end{array}$$

$$\begin{array}{ccc} & S & V \\ \text{The car} & / & \text{crashed against the tree.} \end{array}$$

$$\begin{array}{ccc} & S & V \\ \text{Henry} & / & \text{fished in the river.} \end{array}$$

$$\begin{array}{ccc} & S & V \\ \text{The angry parent} & / & \text{scolded the child.} \end{array}$$

$$\begin{array}{ccc} & S & V \\ \text{That woman} & / & \text{is my friend.} \end{array}$$

$$\begin{array}{ccc} S & & V \\ \text{She} & / & \text{is my friend.} \end{array}$$

$$\begin{array}{ccc} & S & V \\ \text{Everyone} & / & \text{was sorry about the accident.} \end{array}$$

$$\begin{array}{ccc} & S & V \\ \text{The house on the corner} & / & \text{seems bigger than ours.} \end{array}$$

REMEMBER: The complete subject is made up of all the words that tell who or what is doing the action or being spoken about. The simple subject is the main noun or pronoun in the complete subject.

The complete predicate is made up of all the words that tell what the subject does or did or what the subject is or was. The verb is the key word or words in the predicate that express action or state of being.

So far, you have studied only sentences in which the subject comes first and the predicate follows. In Skill Unit 9 you will learn about other sentence patterns.

Apply what you have learned about subjects and verbs by doing the following exercise.

Exercise for Subskill 3A

Divide each sentence into two parts by drawing a line between the complete subject and the complete predicate. Then label the simple subject S and the verb V.

EXAMPLES: The elderly judge / sat in front of the courtroom.

My favorite sweater / is two years old.

1. Lena saves her money.

2. They are our neighbors.

3. The family next door went on a trip.

4. Your friend seems tired tonight.

5. Julia painted the fence.

Check your answers on page 14 in the Answer Key for Book Two. If you correctly identified the parts of all 5 sentences, go to Subskill 3B. If not, do the Supplemental Exercise for Subskill 3A.

Supplemental Exercise for Subskill 3A

Review the information about complete subjects, complete predicates, simple subjects, and verbs on pages 58–61. Then do the following exercise.

Divide each sentence into two parts by drawing a line between the complete subject and the complete predicate. Then label the simple subject S and the verb V.

EXAMPLE: The blue dress on the hanger / is mine.

1. Those children in the park enjoy the new playground equipment.

2. You told them the correct address.

3. Her old car was blue.

4. Those people run in the park every Saturday.

5. Janet is my sister.

Check your answers on page 14 in the Answer Key for Book Two. If you correctly answered 4 of 5 items, go to Subskill 3B. If not, ask your instructor for help.

Subskill 3B: Recognizing Action Verbs

When you complete this subskill, you will be able to recognize action verbs in sentences. If a word can be used as either an action verb or a noun, you will be able to tell when it is being used as a noun and when it is being used as a verb.

Action Verbs

In Subskill 3A you learned that every sentence can be divided into two parts: the complete subject and the complete predicate. You learned that every predicate contains a verb. Remember that verbs can express action or state of being. In this subskill you will learn more about action verbs, or verbs that express action.

Some action verbs are easy to recognize because they express physical action. The action verbs are labeled AV in the following sentences.

> AV
> Marie jumped over the hurdle.

> AV
> Carl ran faster than anyone else.

> AV
> He hit a home run in the third inning.

Other action verbs show mental action.

> AV
> I think about you every day.

> AV
> Their father worries about them.

> AV
> Alice dreamed about you last night.

Action Verb or Noun?

An action verb tells what someone or something does or did.
A noun names a person, place, or thing. Sometimes the same word can
be used as either a verb or a noun. Read the following sentences:

> They <u>paint</u> houses.
>
> They bought the <u>paint</u> at the mall.

In the first sentence, the word <u>paint</u> tells what somebody does. It
is an action verb. In the second sentence, the word <u>paint</u> does not
express an action. It is the name of something. In the second sentence,
the word <u>paint</u> is a noun.

Notice the word <u>the</u> that comes before paint in the second sentence.
That is another clue that <u>paint</u> is used as a noun in that sentence.
Remember that the word <u>the</u> is called a **noun determiner.** When you
see a noun determiner, you can tell that a noun is nearby.

Now look at these two sentences:

> They went to a <u>dance</u>.
>
> They <u>dance</u> well together.

In the first sentence, the word <u>dance</u> is a noun because it tells the
name of something. Another clue that <u>dance</u> is being used as a noun
is that the noun determiner <u>a</u> comes before it. In the second sentence,
the word <u>dance</u> is a verb because it tells what someone does.

Apply what you have learned about action verbs by doing the
following exercises.

Exercise for Subskill 3B

Part A. Each of the following sentences contains an action verb. Underline each action verb.

1. Karen tossed the salad.

2. I wonder about him sometimes.

3. He drives to the store every week.

4. That teacher expects the best from us.

5. We listened carefully to the instructions.

Part B. In each pair of sentences, the underlined word is used once as
a noun and once as a verb. Write <u>N</u> next to the sentence in which the
word is used as a noun. Write <u>V</u> next to the sentence in which the word
is used as a verb.

6. _____ They <u>work</u> at the grocery store.

   _____ Their <u>work</u> is very demanding.

7. ____ She <u>runs</u> two miles every day.

____ Which team had the most <u>runs</u>?

8. ____ He has a nice <u>smile</u>.

____ He <u>smiles</u> at his friends.

9. ____ Brad <u>talks</u> to me at lunch time.

____ The <u>talks</u> were very helpful.

10. ____ That <u>make</u> of automobile is very expensive.

____ They <u>make</u> pumpkin pie for Thanksgiving.

Check your answers on pages 14 and 15 in the Answer Key for Book Two. If you answered all 10 items correctly, go to Subskill 3C. If not, do the Supplemental Exercise for Subskill 3B.

Supplemental Exercise for Subskill 3B

Review the information about action verbs on pages 62 and 63. Then do the following exercise.

Underline the action verbs in the following sentences.

1. Doris paints the house.
2. She walks to school every day.
3. The talks begin tomorrow.
4. Each morning we race to the breakfast table.
5. Howard won the race.
6. The paint spilled all over the floor.
7. We enjoyed the show.
8. They showed me the new typewriter.
9. She dreams of a better future.
10. My dreams came true last week.

Check your answers on page 15 in the Answer Key for Book Two. If you answered 8 of 10 items correctly, go to Subskill 3C. If not, ask your instructor for help.

Subskill 3C: Recognizing Verb Phrases

When you complete this subskill, you will be able to identify verb phrases and to pick out the main verb and helping verbs in a verb phrase.

Verb Phrases

In each of the sentences you have studied so far, the verb has been one word. Sometimes, however, the verb of a sentence is made up of a group of words. A group of words used as a verb is called a **verb phrase.**

A verb phrase consists of a **main verb** plus one or more **helping verbs.** The main verb expresses action or state of being, which you should remember is some form of the word be. It is always the last verb in the phrase.

The following sentences contain verb phrases. In each sentence, the verb phrase has been underlined. Helping verbs are labeled HV. The main verb is labeled MV.

HV HV   MV
They <u>will be working</u> all night.

HV   MV
Roy <u>had driven</u> for an hour.

HV MV
She <u>can study</u> in the library.

The following groups of verbs often serve as helping verbs. Study the chart and memorize the helping verbs.

List of Helping Verbs

<u>be</u> group	<u>have</u> group	<u>do</u> group	other helpers
is	have	do	may
be	has	did	might
am	had	does	must
are			shall
was			should
were			can
been			could
being			will
			would

The following sentences contain helping verbs from all four groups in the chart.

HV MV
They did go to the movies.

HV MV
I might go with them.

HV HV   MV
He has been studying at night school.

HV   MV
The students are learning.

HV MV
The instructor had arrived.

Sometimes the helping verb may be separated from the main verb. Study the verb phrases in the following sentences.

HV   MV
Tim had just begun.

HV   MV
She did not apply for the job.

Apply what you have learned about verb phrases by doing the following exercise.

Exercise for Subskill 3C

Each of the following sentences contains a verb phrase. Look for the group of words that tells what someone or something is doing, will do, or has done. Underline all the words in the verb phrase. Then write <u>MV</u> above the main verb and <u>HV</u> above the helping verbs. You may refer to the list of helping verbs on page 65.

HV MV
EXAMPLE: He <u>had</u> <u>answered</u> the phone.

1.   They will be arriving late.

2.   I will probably be seeing my sister tonight.

3.   The doctor had examined the patient.

4.   We had just finished breakfast.

5.   Linda should not wash the dishes.

6. The police had been questioning the suspect.

7. Mother was baking a cherry pie.

8. The new car did cost a lot of money.

9. She will be receiving Social Security.

10. We may be leaving Monday.

Check your answers on page 15 in the Answer Key for Book Two. If you correctly answered all 10 items, go to Subskill 3D. If not, do the Supplemental Exercise for Subskill 3C.

Supplemental Exercise for Subskill 3C

Review the information about verb phrases on pages 65 and 66. Then do the following exercise.

In each of the following sentences, underline all the words in the verb phrase. Then write MV above the main verb and HV above the helping verbs.

EXAMPLE: We _had_ just _arrived_ at the door.

1. The band was playing in the park.

2. His wife and children will be coming home next week.

3. The team had practiced very hard for the game.

4. Alice has always sent a Christmas card to her friend.

5. I may be applying for a student loan.

6. The tools might have been stored in the garage.

7. You have been elected president of the club.

8. Hank did not donate to the United Fund.

9. We were signing the loan application.

10. Charles can help you with your problem.

Check your answers on pages 15 and 16 in the Answer Key for Book Two. If you correctly answered 8 of 10 items, go to Subskill 3D. If not, ask your instructor for help.

Subskill 3D: Recognizing Linking Verbs

When you complete this subskill, you will be able to identify linking verbs when you see them in sentences.

Linking Verbs

As you learned in Subskill 3A, verbs can do two different kinds of jobs in sentences. Some verbs and verb phrases express action:

> AV
> She went to Florida.

> AV
> She has been going there for years.

Other verbs and verb phrases express a state of being. They link the subject of the sentence to a word in the predicate that identifies or describes the subject. These verbs are called **linking verbs**. The following sentences contain linking verbs or linking verb phrases, which have been labeled LV.

> LV
> She is a doctor.

> LV
> He will be sorry.

> LV
> Mary seems happy.

> LV
> The child is becoming sleepy.

> LV
> They were the owners.

How to Identify Linking Verbs

The most common linking verbs are the forms of the verb <u>be</u>. These are:

am	was	been	be
is	were		being
are			

Other linking verbs include <u>seem</u>, <u>become</u>, <u>appear</u>, <u>prove</u>, <u>look</u>, <u>remain</u>, <u>feel</u>, <u>taste</u>, <u>smell</u>, <u>sound</u>, and <u>grow</u>.

You should memorize these lists of linking verbs. However, you should also know that many of the words on the list are not always linking verbs. Some can be action verbs and some can be helping verbs. The safest way to recognize linking verbs is by looking at how they function in sentences.

A linking verb is like an equal sign in a sentence. It links the subject of the sentence with a word in the predicate that either identifies the subject or describes the subject. Look at the following sentence:

S LV   Identifier
Don is a mechanic.

In this sentence, the noun <u>Don</u> and the noun <u>mechanic</u> name the same person. They are linked by the verb <u>is</u>. The word <u>is</u>, remember, is a form of <u>be</u>. The word <u>is</u> acts like an equal sign in the sentence: Don = mechanic. The word <u>mechanic</u> acts as an identifier. Another word for an identifier is **predicate noun**. Now look at the following sentences. The predicate nouns have been labeled <u>PN</u>.

S   LV   PN
Don has been a mechanic for ten years.

S   LV   PN
Don will be a mechanic soon.

S   LV   PN
Don is becoming a mechanic.

These sentences all contain linking verb phrases. The verb phrases act just like the word <u>is</u> in the first sentence. In each case, the verb phrase acts like an equal sign that links the subject <u>Don</u> to a noun that identifies Don.

Now look at these sentences:

S   LV   Describer
The pie tastes delicious.

S   LV Describer
You seem tired.

```
       S    LV   Describer
      He    is   sorry.
```

```
         S    ___LV___  Describer
      The sky is becoming dark.
```

```
         S      LV    Describer
      That music sounds wonderful.
```

In each of the sentences, a verb or verb phrase links the subject to a word that describes the subject. Words that are placed after a linking verb and describe the subject are called **predicate adjectives**.

REMEMBER: Linking verbs act like equal signs. They link the subject of the sentence to a word in the predicate that identifies or describes the subject. A linking verb may be a single verb or a verb phrase. Common linking verbs include: <u>be</u>, <u>being</u>, <u>been</u>, <u>am</u>, <u>is</u>, <u>are</u>, <u>was</u>, <u>were</u>, <u>seem</u>, <u>become</u>, <u>appear</u>, <u>prove</u>, <u>look</u>, <u>remain</u>, <u>feel</u>, <u>taste</u>, <u>smell</u>, <u>sound</u>, and <u>grow</u>.

Apply what you have learned about linking verbs by doing the following exercise.

Exercise for Subskill 3D

Each sentence below contains a linking verb or linking verb phrase. In each sentence do the following:

- Underline the verb or verb phrase and write <u>LV</u> above it.

- Find the subject of the sentence and write <u>S</u> above it.

- Find the word in the predicate that identifies or describes the subject. Circle that word.

Review your work to be sure that you have completed each step.

```
                 S    LV
EXAMPLE:   Danny will be (captain) of the team.
```

1. Marty seemed successful.

2. The sauce tastes better.

3. Lester will become a carpenter.

4. Sally appears very thin.

5. She has been my friend for a long time.

Check your answers on page 16 in the Answer Key for Book Two. If you correctly answered all 5 items, go on to Subskill 3E. If not, do the Supplemental Exercise for Subskill 3D.

Supplemental Exercise for Subskill 3D

Review the information about linking verbs on pages 68–70. Then do the following exercises.

In each sentence below, do the following:

- Underline the linking verb or linking verb phrase and write LV above it.

- Find the subject of the sentence and write S above it.

- Circle the word in the predicate that identifies or describes the subject.

Review your work to be sure you have completed each step.

EXAMPLE: The band sounded too loud

1. The coffee smells terrific.

2. Dr. Harris has remained a wonderful dentist.

3. Hal has been the leader of our group for many years.

4. Mother will remain strong.

5. The children are growing restless.

Check your answers on page 16 in the Answer Key for Book Two. If you correctly answered 4 of 5 items, go to Subskill 3E. If not, ask your instructor for help.

Subskill 3E: Identifying Linking Verbs and Helping Verbs

When you complete this subskill you will be able to recognize when a be verb is being used as a helping verb and when it is being used as a linking verb.

Be Verbs as Linking Verbs or Helping Verbs

You have learned that the be verbs are be, being, been, am, is, are, was, and were. In Subskill 3C you learned that the be verbs could be used as helping verbs in a verb phrase. In Subskill 3D, you learned that the <u>be</u> verbs could be used as linking verbs. How can you tell when a <u>be</u> verb is being used as a helping verb, and when it is being used as a linking verb?

Study the following sentences:

(1) Ben <u>is</u> going to the store.

(2) Ben <u>is</u> my brother.

In which sentence does the verb <u>is</u> link the subject with a word that identifies the subject? The answer is sentence 2. In sentence 2, <u>is</u> is a linking verb. In which sentence is the verb <u>is</u> part of a verb phrase that expresses action? The answer is sentence 1. In sentence 1, <u>is</u> is a helping verb in the action verb phrase <u>is going</u>.

Now look at these sentences:

```
      S HV    MV   Describer
(1)  I am becoming angry.
       S  HV  MV   Describer
(2)  You are being stubborn.
```

Both sentences contain linking verb phrases. Each verb phrase links the subject with a word that describes the subject. Each verb phrase consists of one main verb and one helping verb. In both sentences, the helping verb is a form of the verb <u>be</u>. In sentence 2, the main verb is also a form of the verb <u>be</u>.

REMEMBER: <u>Be</u> verbs can link the subject to a word in the predicate that identifies or describes the subject. When they do, they are called linking verbs. <u>Be</u> verbs can also act as helping verbs in a verb phrase.

Apply what you have learned about <u>be</u> verbs by doing the following exercise.

Exercise for Subskill 3E

· Underline the verb or verb phrase in each sentence.

· In the blank after each sentence write <u>action</u> if the verb expresses action. Write <u>linking</u> if the verb links the subject to a word that identifies or describes the subject.

· If the sentence has a verb phrase, write MV above the main verb and HV above each helping verb.

Review your work to be sure that you have completed each step.

```
                 HV HV MV
EXAMPLES:  We will be going tomorrow.  _____action_____
```

He <u>was</u> late. _____linking_____

```
              HV  MV
She has been sick.  _____linking_____
```

1. We have been waiting for you. _____

2. You have been a big help. _____

3. Jim was washing his car. _____

4. Mr. Landon will be leading the parade. _____

5. Maria was proud of us. _____

6. She will be the next president. _____

7. We were the winners. _____

8. We were watching the football game. _____

9. I am learning their names. _____

10. I am so surprised! _____

Check your answers on page 16 in the Answer Key for Book Two. If you correctly answered all 10 items, go to Subskill 3F. If not, do the Supplemental Exercise for Subskill 3E.

Supplemental Exercise for Subskill 3E

Review the information about <u>be</u> verbs as helping verbs and linking verbs on pages 71 and 72. Then do the following exercise.

- Underline the verb or verb phrase in each sentence. In the blank after each sentence, write <u>action</u> if the verb expresses action. Write <u>linking</u> if the verb links the subject to a word that identifies or describes the subject.

- If the sentence has a verb phrase, write MV over each main verb and HV over each helping verb.

Review your work to be sure you have completed each step.

EXAMPLES:
              HV HV MV
  He has been trying a new brand.   _____action_____

              HV MV
  You have been very honest.   _____linking_____

1. They will be glad. _____

2. They will be leaving tonight. _____

3. Loretta is reading the newspapers. _____

4. Luis is tired. _____

5. Mark is being so patient! _____

6. Bernadette was telling me a funny story. _____

7. My friend was afraid. _____

8. Angelo will be the first person there.   _____

9. She will be driving the bus.   _____

10. I will be patient.   _____

Check your answers on page 17 in the Answer Key for Book Two. If you correctly answered 8 of 10 items, go to Subskill 3F. If not, ask your instructor for help.

Subskill 3F: Identifying Linking Verbs and Action Verbs

When you complete this subskill, you will be able to recognize when a verb is being used as a linking verb and when it is being used as an action verb.

Verbs as Linking Verbs or Action Verbs

You have learned that action verbs express action. You have learned that linking verbs link the subject to an identifier or describer. The verbs look, feel, taste, smell, sound, and grow can be either linking verbs or action verbs, depending on how they are used in a sentence.

Study the following sentences:

(1)   I smelled the soup.

(2)   The soup smelled delicious.

In sentence 1, the verb smelled expresses an action. It tells what someone did. In sentence 1, smelled is an action verb. In sentence 2, the verb smelled links the subject to a word that describes the subject. In sentence 2, smelled is a linking verb.

Now study these two sentences:

(1)   She looks happy.

(2)   She looks at her watch all day long.

In Sentence 1, the verb looks links the subject to a word that describes the subject. In Sentence 1, the verb looks is a linking verb. In Sentence 2, on the other hand, the verb looks expresses an action. It tells what someone does. In Sentence 2, looks is an action verb.

Apply what you have learned by doing the following exercise.

Exercise for Subskill 3F

Underline the verb in each sentence. In the blank write <u>action</u> if the verb is an action verb. Write <u>linking</u> if the verb is a linking verb.

EXAMPLE: I <u>smell</u> smoke. _____action_____

1. We grew roses in our garden.   _____

2. The children grew tired of the game. _____

3. He is looking at you.   _____

4. He is looking better.   _____

5. That cake tastes delicious.   _____

Check your answers on page 17 in the Answer Key for Book Two. If you correctly answered all 5 items, go the Self-Check on pages 75 and 76. If not, do the Supplemental Exercise for Subskill 3F.

Supplemental Exercise for Subskill 3F

Review the information about words that can be either action verbs or linking verbs on page 74. Then do the following exercise.

Underline the verb in each sentence. In the blank write <u>action</u> if the verb is an action verb. Write <u>linking</u> if the verb is a linking verb.

EXAMPLE: The room <u>smelled</u> smoky. _____linking_____

1. Sam tasted the cake.   _____

2. I felt sick.   _____

3. She felt the satin lining of the coat. _____

4. Someone sounded the fire alarm.   _____

5. That song sounded good.   _____

Check your answers on page 17 in the Answer Key for Book Two. If you correctly answered 4 of 5 items, go to the Self-Check on page 76. If not, ask your instructor for help.

SELF-CHECK: SKILL UNIT 3

Read sentences 1-20 and do the following:

· Underline the verb or verb phrase in each sentence.

· In the blank after each sentence write <u>action</u> if the verb is an action verb. Write <u>linking</u> if the verb is a linking verb.

· If the sentence has a verb phrase, write <u>MV</u> above the main verb and <u>HV</u> above each helping verb.

Review your work to be sure that you have completed each step.

                          HV MV

EXAMPLES: Mario <u>has</u> <u>been</u> a plumber for twenty years.   __linking__

             I <u>felt</u> the sun on my back.   ___action___

1.   Dr. Warminisky is a famous surgeon. ____

2.   Thomas Edison invented the light bulb. ____

3.   That apple pie smells delicious. ____

4.   You look tired today. ____

5.   I have seen the magazine. ____

6.   His work is incredibly dangerous. ____

7.   I am writing this letter to the president of the company. ____

8.   She smelled the new perfume. ____

9.   We have been watching TV. ____

10.   We have been wrong about some things. ____

11.   His father was being patient. ____

12.   Her father was going to Philadelphia. ____

13.   They rushed her to the hospital. ____

14.   I will be working late tonight. ____

15.   The paint on the ceiling was yellow. ____

16.   That water tastes bad. ____

17.   Ethel is looking for you. ____

18.   The child knew the alphabet well. ____

19.   I was thinking about them. ____

20.   The operation was a success. ____

Check your answers on pages 17 and 18 in the Answer Key for Book Two. If you correctly answered 16 of 20 items, you have shown that you have mastered these skills. If not, ask your instructor for help.

Skill Unit 4
USING VERB TENSES CORRECTLY

What Skills You Need to Begin: You need to be able to identify verbs (Skill Unit 3).

What Skills You Will Learn: After studying this skill unit, you will know three of the principal parts of verbs: the present, the past, and the past participle. You will know how to use those parts correctly in order to form the six verb tenses that show time in a sentence.

Why You Need These Skills: You use verbs to tell what happens in a sentence. You also use them to tell whether something happens in the present, the past, or the future. To "tell time" with a verb, you must change the form of the verb. The verb forms that express time are called tenses. Using verb tenses correctly is important for giving accurate information about events. By studying the six verb tenses, you will be able to choose the appropriate form of the verb needed to express any given time relationship in a spoken or written sentence.

How You Will Show What You Have Learned: You will take the Self-Check at the end of this unit on page 92. The Self-Check consists of 15 sentences. If you choose the correct form of the verb needed in 13 of 15 sentences, you will have shown that you have mastered these skills.

If you feel that you have already mastered these skills, turn to the end of this unit and complete the Self-Check on page 92.

Subskill 4A: Using Verbs Correctly in the Present Tense

When you complete this subskill, you will be able to use verbs correctly in the present tense.

Use verbs in the **present tense** to show that something is happening now.

$$\overset{V}{\text{She}}$$

She wants a new coat.

We also use verbs in the present tense to talk about something that often happens.

$$\overset{V}{\text{The block association meets once a month.}}$$

The block association meets once a month.

You also use verbs in the present tense to talk about something that is always true.

$$\overset{V}{\text{Human beings need oxygen to survive.}}$$

Human beings need oxygen to survive.

How to Write Verbs in the Present Tense

In the present tense, a verb has different forms with different subjects. With most subjects, you use the main form of the verb. This is the form found in the dictionary. When the subject is he, she, it, or any singular noun, however, add s or es to the main verb form.

In the following sentences, the verb forms are the same as the main form of the verb walk:

I walk slowly.	They walk slowly.
We walk slowly.	The dogs walk slowly.
You walk slowly.	Julie and Stu walk slowly.

The following sentences show how the verb form changes when the subject is he, she, it, or any singular noun:

He walks slowly.	The dog walks slowly.
She walks slowly.	Julie walks slowly.
It walks slowly.	

The form of the verb that is used with he, she, it, or a singular noun is called the third person singular form. This term will be explained further in Skill Unit 9.

In the above sentences, the verb changes by adding s. When the verb already ends in s, or when the verb ends in x, z, ch, or sh, add es to write the third person singular form of the verb:

We relax on Sundays.	Jerry relaxes on Sundays.
I usually watch TV at night.	She usually watches TV at night.
These fabrics wash easily.	It washes easily.

When a verb ends in a consonant + <u>y</u>, change the <u>y</u> to <u>i</u> before adding <u>es</u>:

They carry the groceries.	My son car<u>ries</u> the groceries.
Those birds fly south in the fall.	That bird <u>flies</u> south in the fall.

Irregular Present Tense Verbs

A few common verbs have present tense forms that do not follow the preceding rules. For this reason, they are sometimes known as **irregular verbs.** All of the helping verbs on the list on page 65 are irregular verbs. You must memorize the present tense forms of these verbs in order to use them correctly.

The verb <u>be</u> is irregular. Look at the following forms of the verb <u>be</u> in the present tense:

I am	he is
we are	she is
you are	it is
they are	(any singular noun) is
(any plural noun) are	

The verbs <u>have</u> and <u>do</u> are also irregular. Look at the following forms of the verbs <u>have</u> and <u>do</u> in the present tense:

I have	he has
we have	she has
you have	it has
they have	(any singular noun) has
(any plural noun) have	

I do	he does
we do	she does
you do	it does
they do	(any singular noun) does
(any plural noun) do	

All other helping verbs never change form. You always use the main form of one of these verbs.

Nat and Stephanie might stop by.	Nat might stop by.
I will see you soon.	She will see you soon.
The stars should be out tonight.	The moon should be out tonight.

Apply what you have learned about using verbs in the present tense by doing the following exercise.

Exercise for Subskill 4A

Write S over the subject of each sentence. Then fill in the blank with the correct present tense form of the verb in parentheses.

EXAMPLE: Her sweater matches her skirt.   (match)

1.   Howard _____ the dishes every night. (dry)

2.   She usually _____ the crossword puzzle in the newspaper.   (do)

3.   You _____ bored.   (seem)

4.   Theresa _____ a new couch.   (have)

5.   Maria _____ her friends from Chicago.   (miss)

6.   Ramon _____ English at the adult education center.   (study)

7.   I _____ worried.   (be)

8.   My friends always _____ basketball on Wednesday nights.   (play)

9.   They _____ some help.   (want)

10.   You _____ the winner.   (be)

11.   Melvin usually _____ his car on Saturday.   (wash)

12.   That tape _____ too much.   (cost)

13.   We _____ one more chance.   (have)

14.   Ralph _____ to work every morning.   (hurry)

15.   You always _____ such good work.   (do)

Check your answers on pages 18 and 19 in the Answer Key for Book Two. If you correctly answered all 15 items, go to Subskill 4B. If not, do the Supplemental Exercise for Subskill 4A.

Supplemental Exercise for Subskill 4A

Review the information about the present tense on pages 77–79. Then do the following exercise.

Write <u>S</u> over the subject of each sentence. Then fill in the blank with the correct present tense form of the verb in parentheses.

                               S
EXAMPLE: The men _____<u>are</u>_____ late.   (be)

1. That product _____ a long time.   (last)

2. You always _____ your share.   (do)

3. The workers _____ on their break.   (be)

4. That outfielder always _____ the fly balls.   (catch)

5. I _____ usually late.   (be)

6. Isabel _____ the heavy bags home by herself.   (carry)

7. Their dog _____ tricks.   (do)

8. You _____ a better job now.   (have)

9. George usually _____ tires on sale.   (buy)

10. She _____ a good idea.   (have)

Check your answers on page 19 in the Answer Key for Book Two. If you correctly answered 8 of 10 items, go to Subskill 4B. If not, ask your instructor for help.

Subskill 4B: Using Verbs Correctly in the Past Tense

When you complete this subskill, you will be able to use the past tense forms of regular and irregular verbs correctly.

The Past Tense

The past tense form of verbs is used to express actions or states of being that began and ended in the past. To form the past tense form of most verbs, you add <u>d</u> or <u>ed</u> to the present. Verbs that form the past tense in this way are called **regular verbs.**

You add <u>d</u> when the present tense form already ends in <u>e</u>. You add <u>ed</u> when the present tense does not end in <u>e</u>.

PRESENT:	look	seem	move	notice
PAST:	looked	seemed	moved	noticed

Spelling Changes in the Past Tense of Regular Verbs

Rule 1: If the present tense form of the verb ends in y, change the y to i, then add ed.

PRESENT:	hurry	rely	try
PAST:	hurried	relied	tried

Rule 2: If a one-syllable word ends in a single vowel plus a single consonant, double the consonant, then add ed, as in the following examples:

PRESENT:	nag	nod	drop
PAST:	nagged	nodded	dropped

Rule 3: If a verb of more than one syllable ends in a single vowel and a single consonant, double the consonant only if there is an accent on the second syllable of the verb. In the following verbs, the accent is on the second syllable, so the consonant is doubled:

PRESENT:	commit	prefer	occur
PAST:	committed	preferred	occurred

In the following verbs, the final syllable is not accented, so you do not double the consonant to form the past:

PRESENT:	benefit	visit
PAST:	benefited	visited

The Past Tense of Irregular Verbs

Some past tense verbs are not formed by adding d or ed to the present. These verbs are irregular. The following verbs are examples of verbs with irregular past tense forms:

PRESENT:	have	do	go	see	come	give	bring	take
PAST:	had	did	went	saw	came	gave	brought	took

The verb be has two past tense forms. Be is the only verb that has a singular form and a plural form in the past tense. Use was with I, he, she, it, and singular nouns. Use were with you, we, they, and plural nouns.

Those police officers were on duty last night.

You were kind to them.

I was sick last week.

The door was locked.

There are many more irregular verbs than the ones listed on page 82. A more complete list appears on pages 101–103. To use irregular verbs correctly in the past tense, you must memorize the past tense forms.

Apply what you have learned about the past tense by doing the following exercise.

Exercise for Subskill 4B

Fill in the blanks with the correct past tense form of the verb in parentheses.

EXAMPLE: The driver ___stopped___ at the red light. (stop)

1. I _____ to her on the phone last night. (talk)

2. We _____ a surprise party for him. (plan)

3. My son _____ asleep. (be)

4. Arnold _____ that movie yesterday. (see)

5. She _____ her best. (do)

6. I _____ the chocolate cake. (prefer)

7. The quarterback _____ the ball in the second half. (drop)

8. They _____ a trip to Puerto Rico. (take)

9. I _____ my nephew a dollar. (give)

10. Marv and Angela _____ out last night. (go)

11. The department store _____ a sale last week. (have)

12. The flood _____ many homes. (destroy)

13. The people on the roller coaster _____. (scream)

14. You _____ right. (be)

15. My mother _____ on the icy sidewalk. (slip)

Check your answers on page 19 in the Answer Key for Book Two. If you correctly answered all 15 items, go to Subskill 4C. If not, do the Supplemental Exercise for Subskill 4B.

Supplemental Exercise for Subskill 4B

Review the information about the past tense on pages 81–83. Then do the following exercise.

Fill in the blanks on page 84 with the correct past tense form of the verb in parentheses.

EXAMPLE: The speaker ___replied___ to the question.   (reply)

1. I _____ to see my friends again.   (hope)

2. The child _____ around on one foot.   (hop)

3. The dishes _____ still in the sink.   (be)

4. My Aunt Irma _____ to visit last week.   (come)

5. We _____ to catch the bus.   (hurry)

6. Mildred _____ up some leftovers.   (heat)

7. Hector _____ his decision later.   (regret)

8. Anna really _____ the program.   (enjoy)

9. They _____ some chicken to the picnic.   (bring)

10. Our friends _____ most of the work.   (do)

11. She _____ on the window to get our attention.   (tap)

12. We _____ tuna casserole for dinner last night.   (have)

13. Rachel _____ a train to Atlanta yesterday.   (take)

14. The hungry baby _____ in her crib.   (cry)

15. I _____ glad to meet your sister last week.   (be)

Check your answers on page 19 in the Answer Key for Book Two. If you correctly answered 12 of 15 items, go to Subskill 4C. If not, ask your instructor for help.

Subskill 4C: Using Verbs Correctly in the Future Tense

When you complete this subskill, you will be able to write the future tense form of verbs correctly.

The Future Tense

The future tense is used to express what will happen or what will be at some time in the future. To form the future tense, use the helping verb <u>will</u> + the present tense of a main verb. Use the main form of the verb, the form without the <u>s</u>.

    PRESENT: You feel dizzy.
    FUTURE: You will feel dizzy.

    PRESENT: Johnson pitches in the seventh inning.
    FUTURE: Johnson will pitch in the seventh inning.

To change a sentence to the future tense, first find the verb. Then change the verb to its main form. Then add <u>will</u> before the verb.

    PAST TENSE: We walked four miles.
    VERB: walked
    MAIN FORM: walk
    FUTURE TENSE: We will walk four miles.

    PRESENT TENSE: Jean watches her step.
    VERB: watches
    MAIN FORM: watch
    FUTURE TENSE: Jean will watch her step.

    PAST TENSE: My uncle had an operation.
    VERB: had
    MAIN FORM: have
    FUTURE TENSE: My uncle will have an operation.

To change a sentence with a form of the verb <u>be</u> to the future tense, always use the word <u>be</u> itself as the main verb.

    PAST TENSE: He was the leader of the band.
    FUTURE TENSE: He will be the leader of the band.

Another Way to Express the Future

Another way to express something that will happen or will be is to use a present tense form of <u>be</u> + the words <u>going to</u>.

I <u>am going to eat</u> dinner later. = I <u>will eat</u> dinner later.
You <u>are going to eat</u> dinner later. = You <u>will eat</u> dinner later.
Jack <u>is going to eat</u> dinner later. = Jack <u>will eat</u> dinner later.
We <u>are going to eat</u> dinner later. = We <u>will eat</u> dinner later.
The boys <u>are going to eat</u> dinner later. = The boys <u>will eat</u>
                                          <u>dinner later.</u>

Apply what you have learned about the future tense by doing the following exercise.

Exercise for Subskill 4C

Each sentence below is in the present tense or the past tense. Read each sentence. Then do the following:

- Underline the verb in the sentence.

- In the blank to the left of the sentence, write <u>present</u> if the verb is in the present tense. Write <u>past</u> if the verb is in the past tense.

- On the first line below the sentence, rewrite the sentence in the future tense, using <u>will</u> + the main form of the main verb.

- On the second line below the sentence, rewrite the sentence in the future tense, using a form of the verb <u>be</u> + <u>going to</u> + the main form of the main verb.

Review your work to be sure that you have completed each step.

EXAMPLE: _____<u>past</u>_____ She <u>slammed</u> the door.

FUTURE: _____She will slam the door._____
_____She is going to slam the door._____

_____ **1.** That cat catches mice.

FUTURE: _____

_____

_____ **2.** Angela did her work carefully.

FUTURE: _____

_____

_____ **3.** I regretted my mistake.

FUTURE: _____

_____

_____ **4.** We enjoy our dinner.

FUTURE: _____

_____

_____ **5.** You were the only person home.

FUTURE: _____

_____

Check your answers on pages 19 and 20 in the Answer Key for Book Two. If you correctly answered all 5 items, go to Subskill 4D. If not, do the Supplemental Exercise for Subskill 4C.

Supplemental Exercise for Subskill 4C

Review the information about the future tense on pages 84 and 85. Then do the following exercise.

Each sentence below is in the present tense or the past tense. Read each sentence. Then do the following:

- Underline the verb in the sentence.

- In the blank to the left of the sentence, write present if the verb is in the present tense. Write past if the verb is in the past tense.

- On the first line below the sentence, rewrite the sentence in the future tense, using will + the main form of the main verb.

- On the second line below the sentence, rewrite the sentence in the future, using a form of the verb be + going to + the main form of the main verb.

Review your work to be sure that you have completed each step.

EXAMPLE: ____past____   I opened the windows.

FUTURE: I will open the windows.
I am going to open the windows.

_____ 1.   The fire fighters want a raise.

FUTURE: _____

_____

_____ 2.   Mel had a good time at the party.

FUTURE: _____

_____

_____ 3.   We relied on you for help.

FUTURE: _____

_____

_____ 4.   I am happy with the results.

FUTURE: _____

_____

_____ 5.   Howard does the laundry.

FUTURE: _____

_____

Check your answers on page 20 in the Answer Key for Book Two. If you correctly answered 4 of 5 items, go to Subskill 4D. If not, ask your instructor for help.

Subskill 4D: Using Past Participles to Form the Perfect Tenses

When you complete this subskill, you will be able to form the past participle of regular verbs. You will also be able to use verbs correctly in the present perfect, the past perfect, and the future perfect tenses.

The three **perfect tenses** all contain a main verb plus one or more helping verbs. The helping verb is always a form of the verb <u>have</u> (<u>have</u>, <u>has</u>, <u>had</u>, or <u>will have</u>). The main verb is always a part called the **past participle.**

Past Participles of Regular Verbs

For regular verbs, the past participle is formed the way the past tense is formed, by adding <u>d</u> or <u>ed</u> to the present.

Present	Past	Past Participle
walk	walked	walked
notice	noticed	noticed
chase	chased	chased
seem	seemed	seemed

Past Participles of Some Irregular Verbs

For irregular verbs, the past participle is not formed by adding <u>d</u> or <u>ed</u> to the present. It is formed in various other ways. The past participle of an irregular verb may not be the same as the past form. When the past participle is different from the past form, you may use the past participle only with a helping verb, usually <u>has</u>, <u>have</u>, or <u>had</u>. The past form of irregular verbs cannot be used with <u>has</u>, <u>have</u>, or <u>had</u>.

The past and past participles of the following verbs are often misused. Study the following examples before reading about the present perfect tense. You will learn more irregular verbs in Skill Unit 5.

Present	Past	Past Participle
am/is/are	was/were	been
do	did	done
go	went	gone
see	saw	seen
have	had	had

The Present Perfect Tense

The **present perfect tense** is formed by using <u>has</u> or <u>have</u> + the past participle of the main verb. Remember that <u>have</u> is used with plural subjects and the pronouns <u>I</u> and <u>you</u>. <u>Has</u> is used with singular subjects.

The **present perfect tense is used to express something that began in the past but continues into the present.** It is also used to talk about something that happened at an indefinite time in the past.

PAST: I <u>lived</u> there last year.
(I used to live there, but I don't anymore.)

PRESENT PERFECT: I <u>have lived</u> here since January.
(I have lived here in the past and I still do.)

PAST: We <u>visited</u> him on Tuesday.
(Sentence tells when the action took place.)

PRESENT PERFECT: We <u>have visited</u> him many times.
(Sentence does not tell when the action took place.)

PAST: I <u>had</u> an egg for breakfast this morning.
(The action was completed in the past.)

PRESENT PERFECT: I <u>have</u> just <u>had</u> an egg.
(The action began in past but is completed in the present.)

Now remember the parts of the verbs <u>do</u>, <u>go</u>, and <u>see</u> you studied on page 88. Notice how the past and past participle forms are used in the following sentences.

PAST: I <u>did</u> all my work last night.
PRESENT PERFECT: I <u>have done</u> all my work.

PAST: She <u>went</u> to the store five minutes ago.
PRESENT PERFECT: She <u>has gone</u> to the store.

PAST: We <u>saw</u> you yesterday.
PRESENT PERFECT: We <u>have seen</u> you many times before.

In each pair of sentences, the first sentence talks about something that happened at a definite time in the past. There is no helping verb in the sentence. That means you need the past form of the verb:

I <u>did</u>   She <u>went</u>   We <u>saw</u>

The second sentence in each pair tells about something that happened at an indefinite time in the past. Each sentence contains the helping verb <u>has</u> or <u>have</u>. That means you need the past participle form of the verbs. Remember, the past participle is the form of the verb used with <u>has</u> or <u>have</u>. Do not use the past participle without a helping verb:

I <u>have done</u>　　She <u>has gone</u>　　We <u>have seen</u>

The Past Perfect Tense

The **past perfect tense** is formed by using the helping verb <u>had</u> + the past participle of the main verb. This tense **is used to show that one past action took place before another past action.**

> I <u>had worked</u> there for two years before they finally gave me a raise.
>
> I <u>had</u> already <u>seen</u> the program, so I turned off the television.
>
> I <u>had had</u> enough to eat, so I left the table.

The Future Perfect Tense

The **future perfect tense** is formed by using the helping verbs <u>will have</u> + the past participle of the main verb. This tense **is used to show that an action will be completed by or before a certain time in the future.** It is often used to show that one action will be completed before another takes place.

> By next week we <u>will have learned</u> all the rules.
>
> Before January, she <u>will have saved</u> enough money.
>
> By the time you return, the girls <u>will have raked</u> all the leaves.
>
> By the end of this month, we <u>will have had</u> a record amount of rain.

Apply what you have learned about the perfect tenses by doing the following exercise.

Exercise for Subskill 4D

Each of the following sentences is written in the past tense. On the lines given, rewrite the sentence in the present perfect, the past perfect, and the future perfect tenses.

EXAMPLE:　I watched TV for an hour.

PRES. PERF.:　I have watched TV for an hour.

PAST PERF.:　I had watched TV for an hour.

FUT. PERF.:　I will have watched TV for an hour.

1. Al went to Philadelphia.

PRES. PERF.: _____

PAST PERF.: _____

FUT. PERF.: _____

2. We carried the injured man to safety.

PRES. PERF.: _____

PAST PERF.: _____

FUT. PERF.: _____

3. I saw the movie twice.

PRES. PERF.: _____

PAST PERF.: _____

FUT. PERF.: _____

4. My parents stayed with me.

PRES. PERF.: _____

PAST PERF.: _____

FUT. PERF.: _____

5. He did all the laundry.

PRES. PERF.: _____

PAST PERF.: _____

FUT. PERF.: _____

Check your answers on page 20 in the Answer Key for Book Two. If you correctly answered all 5 items, go to the Self-Check. If not, do the Supplemental Exercise for Subskill 4D.

Supplemental Exercise for Subskill 4D

Review the information about the perfect tenses on pages 88–90. Then do the following exercise.

Each of the sentences on page 92 is written in the past tense. On the lines given, rewrite the sentence in the present perfect, the past perfect, and the future perfect tenses.

EXAMPLE: We waited patiently for the train.

PRES. PERF.:   We have waited patiently for the train.

PAST PERF.:   We had waited patiently for the train.

FUT. PERF.:   We will have waited patiently for the train.

1. Miguel saw the parade.

    PRES. PERF.:   _____

    PAST PERF.:   _____

    FUT. PERF.:   _____

2. We listened to the entire speech.

    PRES. PERF.:   _____

    PAST PERF.:   _____

    FUT. PERF.:   _____

3. Those women did me a favor.

    PRES. PERF.:   _____

    PAST PERF.:   _____

    FUT. PERF.:   _____

4. Something went wrong.

    PRES. PERF.:   _____

    PAST PERF.:   _____

    FUT. PERF.:   _____

5. She had two operations on her heart.

    PRES. PERF.:   _____

    PAST PERF.:   _____

    FUT. PERF.:   _____

Check your answers on pages 20 and 21 in the Answer Key for Book Two. If you correctly answered 4 of 5 items, go to the Self-Check. If not, ask your instructor for help.

SELF-CHECK: SKILL UNIT FOUR

Underline the correct verb form needed in each sentence.

EXAMPLE: She (holded, held) my hand.

1. That movie (last, lasts) too long.

2. They (saw, seen) a fire truck on their block.

3. My friend (do, does) a lot of favors for me.

4. I (be going to, am going to) the store.

5. The lights have (went, gone) out.

6. Jack (has, have) tried out his new fishing rod.

7. By tonight we will have (lose, lost) five games.

8. You (was, were) trying too hard.

9. Those men (likes, like) the food in the coffee shop.

10. Winston always (drop, drops) the ball.

11. Les and Anita (watch, watches) basketball games on Saturday.

12. Joan (wash, washes) her hair every day.

13. Will you (came, come) to my party?

14. Sue and David (gone, went) to the movies.

15. The hiking party will (walk, walked) five miles.

Check your answers on page 21 in the Answer Key for Book Two. If you correctly answered 12 of 15 items, you have shown that you have mastered these skills. If not, ask your instructor for help.

Skill Unit 5
USING PROGRESSIVE FORMS AND IRREGULAR VERBS

What Skills You Need to Begin: You need to be able to identify and use nouns (Units 1 and 2), identify verbs (Unit 3), and identify verb tenses and use them correctly (Unit 4).

What Skills You Will Learn: When you complete this skill unit, you will know what is meant by "principal parts of verbs." You will be able to identify and use the six progressive forms of verb tenses correctly. You will be able to use the past and past participle forms of irregular verbs correctly. You will also be able to choose the correct verb to use from certain frequently confused verbs.

Why You Need These Skills: You have learned how to use the perfect tenses to show that one action has taken place before another, or that one action will take place after another. The perfect tenses of a verb are formed by using a helping verb with the past participle of the main verb. Sometimes you will also need to show whether an event is in progress, whether it has already stopped, or whether it will continue for some time to come. Knowing how to use **progressive forms** of verb tenses will allow you to describe an action in progress in the past, the present and the future. Irregular verbs are those that form some tenses in unusual ways. Standard English requires that you use the correct forms of irregular verbs. Also, there are some sets of verbs that are frequently confused. If you learn the meanings of these verbs and when to use them, you won't confuse the people who hear you speak or read what you write.

How You Will Show What You Have Learned: You will take the Self-Check at the end of this unit on page 113. The Self-Check consists of 15 sentences. If you choose the correct form of the verb needed in 13 of 15 sentences, you will have shown that you have mastered these skills.

If you feel that you have already mastered these skills, turn to the end of this unit and complete the Self-Check on page 113.

Subskill 5A: Using the Progressive Forms of Tenses Correctly

When you complete this subskill, you will be able to use the six progressive forms of verb tenses correctly.

Progressive Verb Forms

Each of the six verb tenses has a progressive form. **The progressive form of a verb tense is used to show that an action is in progress or continuing at the time referred to in the sentence.** A progressive verb form consists of a form of the verb <u>be</u> and the <u>ing</u> form of the main verb. The <u>ing</u> form of a verb is called its **present participle**. The following examples show the progressive form for each of the six verb tenses.

PRESENT TENSE:	The mechanic <u>works</u> on the car.
PRESENT PROGRESSIVE:	The mechanic <u>is working</u> on the car right now.
	I <u>am working</u> on the car right now.
	They <u>are working</u> on the car right now.

The present progressive uses the helping verb <u>am</u>, <u>is</u>, or <u>are</u> and the present participle.

PAST TENSE:	The mechanic <u>worked</u> on the car.
PAST PROGRESSIVE:	The mechanic <u>was working</u> on the car when the phone rang.
	The mechanics <u>were working</u> on the car when the phone rang.

The past progressive uses the helping verb <u>was</u> or <u>were</u> and the present participle.

FUTURE TENSE:	The mechanic <u>will work</u> on the car.
FUTURE PROGRESSIVE:	The mechanic <u>will be working</u> on the car this morning.

The future progressive uses the helping verbs <u>will be</u> and the present participle.

PRESENT PERFECT:	The mechanic <u>has worked</u> on the car.
PRESENT PERFECT PROGRESSIVE:	The mechanic <u>has been working</u> on the car most of the day.
	The mechanics <u>have been working</u> on the car most of the day.

The present perfect progressive uses the helping verbs <u>has been</u> or <u>have been</u> and the present participle.

PAST PERFECT:	The mechanic <u>had worked</u> on the car.
PAST PERFECT PROGRESSIVE:	The mechanic <u>had been working</u> on the car for three hours before he went to lunch.

The past perfect progressive uses the helping verbs <u>had been</u> and the present participle.

FUTURE PERFECT:	The mechanic <u>will have worked</u> on the car.
FUTURE PERFECT PROGRESSIVE:	The mechanic <u>will have been working</u> on the car for a week by the time we get it back.

The future perfect progressive uses the helping verbs <u>will have been</u> and the present participle.

Spelling the <u>-ing</u> Form of Verbs

Rule 1:   For most verbs, simply add <u>-ing</u> to the present tense.

wait + ing = waiting

stand + ing = standing

Rule 2:   For verbs that end with silent <u>e</u> preceded by a consonant, drop the final <u>e</u> before adding <u>-ing</u>.

take + ing = taking

ride + ing = riding

Rule 3:   If a one syllable verb ends in a single consonant with a single vowel right before it, double the final consonant before adding -ing.

> plan + ing = planning
>
> let + ing = letting

Rule 4:   If a verb of more than one syllable ends in a single consonant with a single vowel right before it, double the final consonant only if the stress is on the final syllable. Do not double the consonant if the stress is not on the final syllable.

> begin + ing = beginning
>
> prefer + ing = preferring
>
> commit + ing = committing
>
> forget + ing = forgetting
>
> BUT: benefit + ing = benefiting
>
> visit + ing = visiting

Rule 5:   Never double a final x, y, or w.

> relax + ing = relaxing
>
> enjoy + ing = enjoying
>
> row + ing = rowing

Changing a Verb to Its Progressive Form

Remember that the -ing form of the verb is made from the present tense. To change a verb to its progressive form, use a form of be plus the -ing form of the main verb. Remember to change the main verb to its present tense form before adding -ing.

> I go to the park.   (present)
> I am going to the park.   (present progressive)
>
> I went to the park.   (past)
> I was going to the park.   (past progressive)
>
> Frank has told me the truth.   (present perfect)
> Frank has been telling me the truth.
> (present perfect progressive)

The Principal Parts of a Verb

The present form, past form, past participle, and present participle of a verb are known as its principal parts. The following chart lists the principal parts of some regular verbs:

Present	Past	Past Participle	Present Participle
walk	walked	walked	walking
notice	noticed	noticed	noticing
chase	chased	chased	chasing
seem	seemed	seemed	seeming
live	lived	lived	living
drag	dragged	dragged	dragging

Knowing the principal parts of regular verbs allows you to form the progressive tenses correctly. In the next subskill, we will examine the principal parts of irregular verbs and learn how to use them to form progressive tenses.

Apply what you have learned about the progressive tenses by doing the following exercise.

Exercise for Subskill 5A

In each of the following sentences, underline the correct helping verb of each pair in parentheses. Then fill in the blank with the progressive form of the verb in parentheses under the blank.

EXAMPLE: I (have been, <u>will have been</u>) _____working_____ on the re-
                                                        (work)

port by the time you arrive tomorrow.

1. I (have, am) _____ the clothes now.
              (wash)

2. They (have been, will have been) _____ in Detroit for
                                            (live)

the past several months.

3. We (are, had been) _____ the game when Adam
                              (win)

twisted his ankle.

4. During the last game, the players (were, have been)

_____ many fouls.
   (commit)

5. When I saw Emily earlier today, she (was, has been)

_____ out the window.
   (stare)

6. Tomorrow, Hank (had been, will be) _____ new
                       (buy)

clothes.

7. When Sheila arrived, Cynthia (will be, had been)

_____ for two hours.
   (study)

8. By the time the coach gets here, the team (had been, will have

been)_____ long enough.
     (practice)

9. Rita was frustrated because she (will be, had been)

_____ a long time for the bus.
   (wait)

10. Several people (were, will be) _____ for the meeting
                    (arrive)

when you called.

Check your answers on page 21 in the Answer Key for Book Two.
If you correctly answered all 10 items, go to Subskill 5B. If not, do the
Supplemental Exercise for Subskill 5A.

Supplemental Exercise for Subskill 5A

Review the information about the progressive tenses on pages 95–
98. Then do the following exercise.

In each of the following sentences, underline the correct helping verb of each pair in parentheses. Then fill in the blank with the progressive form of the verb in parentheses under the blank.

EXAMPLE: Melvin (will be, <u>had been</u>) ____sleeping____ when I called.
              (sleep)

1. During her vacation next month, Rachel (will be, was)

    _____ some friends.
        (visit)

2. We (were, have been) _____ in the lake when it
                             (swim)
    started to rain.

3. In the morning, Dora could see that it (was, had been)

    _____ all night.
        (rain)

4. Your parents (had been, will be) _____ soon.
                                       (arrive)

5. Our neighbors told me they (are, will have been)

    _____ about moving.
        (think)

6. We were exhausted because we (were, had been) _____
                                                      (drive)
    for ten hours.

7. He (will be, was) _____ the locks first thing tomorrow
                         (change)
    morning.

8. Before they move, they (will be, had been) _____ all
                                                  (sell)
    their furniture.

9. Helen (will have been, had been) _____ for six hours
                                        (study)
    by the time Peter arrived.

10. Harold (was, will be) _____ for the red light when a
                            (stop)
    car sped past him.

Check your answers on page 21 in the Answer Key for Book Two. If you correctly answered 8 of 10 items, go to Subskill 5B. If not, ask your instructor for help.

Subskill 5B: Using the Past and Past Participle Forms of Irregular Verbs Correctly

When you complete this subskill, you will be able to use the past and past participle forms of irregular verbs correctly.

The Principal Parts of Irregular Verbs

As you have learned, the present, the past, and the past participle forms of a verb are used to form the six tenses of the verb. The **present participle is used to form the progressive forms of verb tenses.** These forms are known as the principal parts of verbs.

You have learned that most verbs are regular verbs. The past and past participles of regular verbs are both formed by adding d or ed to the present form. However, many verbs are irregular. The past and past participles of irregular verbs are not formed by adding d or ed. Some irregular verbs have different forms for the past and past participles. Other irregular verbs have the same form for the past and past participle. To use irregular verbs correctly, you will have to memorize the principal parts of as many verbs as possible. You should always look up the principal parts in a dictionary if you are not sure of what they are.

The following charts contain the most common irregular verbs. These charts do not list the present participles of irregular verbs. The present participles of all verbs are formed by adding ing to the present.

Present	Past	Past Participle
bend	bent	bent
bleed	bled	bled
bring	brought	brought
catch	caught	caught
cling	clung	clung
creep	crept	crept
dig	dug	dug
fight	fought	fought
feel	felt	felt
find	found	found
get	got	got, gotten

Present	Past	Past Participle
hold	held	held
lead	led	led
leave	left	left
lend	lent	lent
lose	lost	lost
mean	meant	meant
pay	paid	paid
say	said	said
sell	sold	sold
send	sent	sent
shoot	shot	shot
sleep	slept	slept
slide	slid	slid
speed	sped	sped
spend	spent	spent
stand	stood	stood
strike	struck	struck
swing	swung	swung
teach	taught	taught
tell	told	told
weep	wept	wept
wind	wound	wound
wring	wrung	wrung

Several irregular verbs have the same form for all their parts. Practice saying and spelling them until they also become familiar.

Present	Past	Past Participle
bet	bet, betted	bet
burst	burst	burst
cost	cost	cost
hurt	hurt	hurt
let	let	let
put	put	put
quit	quit	quit
shut	shut	shut

For other irregular verbs, the past and past participle forms are different. Study the principal parts of these verbs until you know them well. You will know them well when you can correctly spell all three parts.

Present	Past	Past Participle
beat	beat	beaten, beat
become	became	become
begin	began	begun
bite	bit	bitten

Present	Past	Past Participle
blow	blew	blown
break	broke	broken
choose	chose	chosen
come	came	come
do	did	done
draw	drew	drawn
drink	drank	drunk
drive	drove	driven
eat	ate	eaten
fall	fell	fallen
fly	flew	flown
forget	forgot	forgotten
forgive	forgave	forgiven
freeze	froze	frozen
give	gave	given
grow	grew	grown
hide	hid	hidden
know	knew	known
ride	rode	ridden
ring	rang	rung
run	ran	run
shake	shook	shaken
shrink	shrank	shrunk
sing	sang	sung
sink	sank	sunk
speak	spoke	spoken
steal	stole	stolen
swear	swore	sworn
swim	swam	swum
take	took	taken
tear	tore	torn
wear	wore	worn
write	wrote	written

Finding Principal Parts in a Dictionary

If you do not know the principal parts of a verb, you can look them up in a dictionary. To find the principal parts of a verb in the dictionary, look up the present tense form of the verb. After the present tense form and its pronunciation, you will sometimes find three other words in dark type. These words are the principal parts of that verb. The first word in dark type is the past form of the verb. The second word in dark type is the past participle, and the third word is the present participle. When the past and past participle are the same, the word is given only once. Some dictionaries list the principal parts of irregular verbs only. If your dictionary does not list the principal parts of a verb, you know that the verb is a regular verb.

Look at the dictionary entries on the following page.

ask (ask) *vt.* [OE. *ascian*] **1.** to use words in seeking the answer to (a question) **2.** to put a question to (a person) **3.** to request or demand **4.** to invite —*vi.* **1.** to make a request (*for*) **2.** to inquire (*about*)

break (brāk) *vt.* **broke, bro′ken, break′ing** [OE. *brecan*] **1.** to split or crack into pieces by force; smash **2.** to cut open the surface of (soil, the skin, etc.) **3.** to make fail or end by force [to *break* a strike] **4.** to make useless as by cracking or shattering **5.** to tame as with force **6.** *a)* to cause to get rid (*of* a habit) *b)* to get rid of (a habit) **7.** to demote **8.** to make poor or bankrupt **9.** to surpass (a record) **10.** to violate, as a law **11.** to disrupt [to *break* ranks] **12.** to interrupt (a journey, electric circuit, etc.) **13.** to lessen the force of, as a fall, by interrupting **14.** to end suddenly, as a tie score **15.** to penetrate, as darkness **16.** to disclose **17.** to decipher or solve —*vi.* **1.** to split into pieces **2.** to force one's way (*through*) **3.** to stop associating (*with*) **4.** to become useless or ruined **5.** to change suddenly [his voice *broke*] **6.** to begin suddenly [*break* into song] **7.** to become disclosed **8.** to stop activity temporarily **9.** to fall apart or collapse —*n.* **1.** a breaking **2.** a broken place **3.** a beginning to appear [the *break* of day] **4.** an interruption of regularity **5.** an interval, gap, or rest **6.** a sudden change **7.** an escape **8.** [Slang] a piece of luck —**break down 1.** to go out of working order **2.** to collapse physically or emotionally **3.** to analyze —**break in 1.** to enter forcibly **2.** to interrupt **3.** to train (a beginner) **4.** to get the stiffness out of —**break off** to stop abruptly —**break out 1.** to escape **2.** to get pimples or a rash —**break up 1.** to separate; disperse **2.** to stop **3.** [Colloq.] to distress **4.** [Colloq.] to laugh or make laugh —**break′a·ble** *adj.*

catch (kach) *vt.* **caught, catch′ing** [< L. *capere*, to take] **1.** to seize and hold; capture **2.** to take by a trap **3.** to deceive **4.** to surprise **5.** to get to in time [to *catch* a bus] **6.** to lay hold of; grab [to *catch* a ball] **7.** to become infected with [to *catch* a cold] **8.** to understand **9.** to get entangled **10.** [Colloq.] to see, hear, etc. —*vi.* **1.** to become held, fastened, etc. **2.** to burn **3.** to keep hold, as a lock —*n.* **1.** a catching **2.** a thing that catches **3.** something caught **4.** one worth catching as a spouse **5.** a break in the voice **6.** [Colloq.] a tricky qualification —**catch at** to reach for eagerly —**catch on 1.** to understand **2.** to become popular —**catch up 1.** to snatch **2.** to overtake

The entry for <u>ask</u> has no words in dark type after the present form. This is because <u>ask</u> is a regular verb. You know, then, that both the past and past participle forms of <u>ask</u> are <u>asked</u>. The present participle is <u>asking</u>.

The entry for the verb <u>break</u> gives all the principal parts of the verb. The past is <u>broke</u>, the past participle is <u>broken</u>, and the present participle is <u>breaking</u>.

The dictionary lists only two principal parts for the verb <u>catch</u>: <u>caught</u> and <u>catching</u>. Remember that when the past and past participle forms of a verb are the same, the dictionary lists the form only once. You can tell from the entry for <u>catch</u> that the past and past participle are both <u>caught</u>. The present participle is <u>catching</u>.

Exercise for Subskill 5B

Part A. Complete the following chart by filling in the past and past participle forms of the verbs listed. If you can't remember the parts, look them up in the table in this unit or in your dictionary.

EXAMPLE: sing   _____ sing _____   _____ sang _____

Present	Past	Past Participle
1. lose	_____	_____
2. know	_____	_____
3. see	_____	_____
4. ride	_____	_____
5. do	_____	_____
6. break	_____	_____
7. stand	_____	_____
8. fly	_____	_____
9. bite	_____	_____
10. hold	_____	_____
11. speak	_____	_____
12. forgive	_____	_____
13. eat	_____	_____
14. drink	_____	_____
15. catch	_____	_____

Part B. Fill in the blanks in sentences 16-25 with either the past or the past participle form of the verb in parentheses.

EXAMPLE: We have   _____ sung _____   that song many times. (sing)

16. She _____ her arm in an accident last year. (break)

17. The birds have _____ south for the winter. (fly)

18. I have _____ about that for a long time. (know)

19. She has already _____ her breakfast. (eat)

20. I _____ my keys last night. (lose)

21. Jane _____ Niagara Falls at sunset. (see)

22. The dog had _____ through the collar. (bite)

23. By tomorrow they will have _____ three meetings. (hold)

24. My husband _____ me for hurting his feelings. (forgive)

25. The doctor _____ everything he could to save the man. (do)

Check your answers on page 22 in the Answer Key for Book Two. If you correctly answered all 25 items, go to Subskill 5C. If not, do the Supplemental Exercise for Subskill 5B.

Supplemental Exercise for Subskill 5B

Review the principal parts of the irregular verbs on pages 101–104. Then do the following exercise.

Part A. Complete the following chart by filling in the past and past participle forms of the verbs listed. If you can't remember the parts, look them up in the table in this unit or in your dictionary.

EXAMPLE: bend   <u>bent</u>   <u>bent</u>

	Present	Past	Past Participle
1.	put	_____	_____
2.	let	_____	_____
3.	spend	_____	_____
4.	bring	_____	_____
5.	teach	_____	_____
6.	lend	_____	_____
7.	drive	_____	_____
8.	throw	_____	_____
9.	quit	_____	_____
10.	sell	_____	_____
11.	come	_____	_____
12.	take	_____	_____
13.	swim	_____	_____
14.	choose	_____	_____
15.	find	_____	_____

Part B. Fill in the blanks in sentences 16-25 with either the past or the past participle form of the verb in parentheses.

EXAMPLE: The man ____<u>bent</u>____ down to pick up the coin.   (bend)

16. My brother had _____ me some money.   (lend)

17. They have _____ a new leader.   (choose)

18. I _____ my job last week. (quit)

19. We had _____ to the end of our trip. (come)

20. My friend _____ me how to drive. (teach)

21. Jessie _____ her old furniture. (sell)

22. I _____ a vacation last July. (take)

23. Someone had _____ all the air out of the tires. (let)

24. She _____ a dollar in her coat pocket. (find)

25. No one had _____ a camera to the wedding. (bring)

Check your answers on pages 22 and 23 in the Answer Key for Book Two. If you correctly answered 20 of 25 items, go to Subskill 5C. If not, ask your instructor for help.

Subskill 5C: Using Some Problem Verbs Correctly

When you complete this subskill, you will be able to use the verbs sit and set, lie and lay, rise and raise, let and leave, teach and learn, and used to and supposed to correctly.

There are five pairs of verbs that are often misused. Sometimes the verbs are misused because people forget the principal parts. More often, the verbs are misused because people are confused about what they mean. If you understand the correct meanings of these verbs, you will use them correctly in your speech and writing.

"Lie" and "Lay"

Lie means "to rest, to recline, or be situated." The principal parts are lie, lay, lain.

PRESENT:	Lie down, Spot! I lie down every afternoon.
PAST:	I lay down for a nap yesterday.
PAST PARTICIPLE:	My books have lain on the table all night.

Lay means "to put or place something." It is followed by a word that tells what was put or placed. The principal parts are lay, laid, laid.

PRESENT:	Lay your books on the table.
PAST:	I laid my books on the table.
PAST PARTICIPLE:	I have always laid my books on the table.

"Sit" and "Set"

Sit means "to take a seat" or "to be situated." The principal parts are sit, sat, sat.

PRESENT:	I often sit in my favorite chair after a hard day's work.
	The house sits on two acres of land.
PAST:	I sat in my chair yesterday.
PAST PARTICIPLE:	I have always sat in my favorite chair.

Set means "to put or place something." It is usually followed by a word that tells what was set. The principal parts are set, set, set.

PRESENT:	I usually set the groceries on the table as soon as I get home.
PAST:	I set the groceries on the table last night.
PAST PARTICIPLE:	I have just set the groceries on the table.

"Rise" and "Raise"

Rise means "to get up" or "to move higher." The principal parts are rise, rose, risen.

PRESENT:	The price of food rises often.
	I rise each morning at six.
PAST:	I rose yesterday at six.
PAST PARTICIPLE:	I have risen at six for many years.

Raise means "to lift an object" or "to increase something." The verb is followed by a word that tells what was raised. The principal parts are raised, raised, raised.

PRESENT:	I raise the window before I cook.
PAST:	I raised the window yesterday.
	The company raised my wages.
PAST PARTICIPLE:	I have raised the window many times.

"Teach" and "Learn"

Teach means "to show how" or "to give instruction." A person who gives instruction teaches something. The principal parts are teach, taught, taught.

PRESENT: I teach swimming every summer.

PAST: I taught swimming last summer.
                      She taught me the song.

PAST PARTICIPLE: I have taught swimming for several summers.

Learn means "to find out about something." A person who receives instruction learns something. The principal parts are learn, learned, learned.

PRESENT: I learn something new every day.

PAST: I learned something new yesterday.

PAST PARTICIPLE: I have always learned something new.

"Let" and "Leave"

Let means "to allow" or "to permit." The principal parts are let, let, let.

PRESENT: Let me help.
                      I let him borrow my car whenever his breaks down.

PAST: I let him borrow my car yesterday.

PAST PARTICIPLE: I have let him borrow my car many times.

Leave means "to go away" or "to cause something to remain." The principal parts are leave, left, left.

PRESENT: Leave it here.
                      I leave for work at seven.

PAST: I left for work at seven yesterday.
                      I left it at home.

PAST PARTICIPLE: I have always left for work at seven.
                      She had left her keys in the ignition.

NOTE: Some problems with let and leave are associated with certain common phrases. Study the examples of correct usage on page 110.

<u>Let</u> her be.
(Allow her to be the way she wants to be.)

<u>Let</u> her alone.
(Allow her to be alone.)

OR: <u>Leave</u> her alone.
(Go away and leave her where she is.)

"Supposed to" and "Used to"

The expressions <u>supposed to</u> and <u>used to</u> use the past or past participle form of the verb, not the present tense form. Be sure there is a <u>d</u> at the end of each verb.

We are <u>supposed</u> to bring our children.

I am <u>used</u> to driving that kind of car.

She <u>used</u> to visit us more often.

Apply what you have learned about troublesome verbs by doing the following exercise.

Exercise for Subskill 5C

Part A.   Above each of the following sentences are the principal parts of one or two verbs. In each blank, write the verb form that correctly completes each sentence.

EXAMPLE: lie lay lain   lay laid laid

The patient had <u>lain</u> on the operating table for two hours.
I <u>laid</u> some new tile in the kitchen over the weekend.

rise   rose   risen   raise   raised   raised

1.   My hopes have _____ since I received the letter.

2.   The letter _____ my hopes yesterday.

let   let   let   leave   left   left

3.   Why won't you _____ us help you?

4.   I _____ my keys at home.

lie   lay   lain   lay   laid   laid

5.   _____ down and take a nap.

6.   Do you plan to _____ the money away to buy a television set?

learn   learned   learned   teach   taught   taught

7. My friend _____ me how to sew last year.

8. I _____ my new job quickly and was congratulated by my boss.

suppose   supposed   supposed

9. We were _____ to meet in front of the bank.

use   used   used

10. Randy _____ to work for the city's water department.

Part B. Underline the correct verb choice in each sentence.

EXAMPLE: He (leaved, <u>left</u>) this morning at eight.

11. That store (raised, rose) its prices again.

12. I forgot where I (layed, laid) the hammer.

13. (Lie, Lay) down and take a rest.

14. (Let, Leave) me be!

15. Who (learned, taught) you to do that?

16. The cake did not (raise, rise) well.

17. (Set, Sit) down and make yourself comfortable.

18. He (laid, lay) down for a nap an hour ago.

19. (Set, Sit) your keys on the mantle.

20. You are (suppose, supposed) to set a good example.

Check your answers on page 23 in the Answer Key for Book Two. If you correctly answered all 20 items, go to the Self-Check. If not, do the Supplemental Exercise for Subskill 5C.

Supplemental Exercise for Subskill 5C

Review the information about verbs that are often misused on pages 107–110. Then do the following exercise.

Part A. Above each of the following sentences are the principal parts of one or two verbs. In each blank, write the verb form that correctly completes each sentence.

EXAMPLE: learn   learned   learned   teach   taught   taught

The woman who ___taught___ me to drive was extremely aware of safety.
Was it easy for you to ___learn___ geometry?

      lie   lay   lain   lay   laid   laid

1. Where did you _____ the green book?

2. I am going to _____ down for an hour.

      rise   rose   risen   raise   raised   raised

3. She _____ early yesterday to get to an important meeting.

4. They still have to _____ the roof on the house they are building.

      sit   sat   sat   set   set   set

5. _____ the roses over there in the corner.

6. These boxes have _____ there all week.

      leave   left   left   let   let   let

7. It's unsafe to _____ young children alone even for a short time.

8. Did you _____ them go to the movies Saturday afternoon?

      use   used   used

9. We _____ to take a drive in the country on Sundays.

      suppose   supposed   supposed

10. Hank was _____ to study algebra this semester.

Part B. Underline the correct verb in each sentence.

EXAMPLE: The sun (<u>rises</u>, raises)   earlier in the summer.

11. The car has (set, sat)   in the driveway for weeks.

12. She (set, sat)   down in the most comfortable chair.

13. I (leaved, left)   my book at home.

14. Mabel (teaches, learns)   people how to dance.

15. (Let, Leave)   the children go outside.

16. He (use, used)   to drive a cab.

17. The company (raised, rose)   everybody's wages.

18. Those dirty socks have (laid, lain)   there for days.

19. The dog always (lies, lays)   down in front of the TV.

20. Frank (set, sat)   the glass down on the counter.

Check your answers on pages 23 and 24 in the Answer Key for Book Two. If you correctly answered all 20 items, go to the Self-Check. If not, ask your instructor for help.

SELF-CHECK: SKILL UNIT 5

Underline the correct verb form needed in each sentence.

EXAMPLE: My friend   (teach, <u>taught</u>)   me how to drive.

1. We have already   (ate, eaten).
2. As soon as I   (lay, laid)   down, I fell asleep.
3. The baby had   (torn, tore)   the pages of the book.
4. Mel   (learned, taught)   me how to play poker.
5. (Set, Sit)   the cans on the shelf.
6. I have   (took, taken)   a picture of them.
7. Tim   (brung, brought)   me some flowers.
8. You have been   (forgeting, forgetting)   things lately.
9. The smoke   (rise, rose)   into the air.
10. She   (did, done)   the right thing.
11. What is   (takeing, taking)   them so long.
12. (Lie, Lay)   down for a few minutes if you are tired.
13. He was   (suppose, supposed)   to be here by now.
14. The owner of the land   (let, letted)   us skate on the lake.
15. I   (used, use)   to drive my father's car before he sold it.

Check your answers on page 24 in the Answer Key for Book Two. If you correctly answered 12 of 15 items, you have shown that you have mastered these skills. If not ask your instructor for help.

Neither man could see the train.

Man is a noun. Neither answers "Which man?" Neither is used as an adjective.

Many people saw the performance.

People is a noun. Many answers "How many people?" Many is used as an adjective.

NOTE: When the noun is taken out, these words become pronouns.

COMPARE: Neither man knew the way.   (adjective)

Neither knew the way.   (pronoun)

COMPARE: Each girl did her best.   (adjective)

Each did her best.   (pronoun)

(2)   The possessive pronouns my, your, her, its, their, and our are always used as adjectives.

She has improved her score.

The adjective her modifies the noun score. It tells "Which one?"

They are eating their lunches.

The adjective their modifies the noun lunches.

The word his can be used as either an adjective or a pronoun. When his is used as the subject of a sentence, it is a pronoun. When his comes right before a noun, it is an adjective.

ADJECTIVE: His hamburger was well done.

PRONOUN: His was well done.

The words mine, hers, ours, and theirs never come right before a noun. When they are the subjects of sentences, they are being used as pronouns.

ADJECTIVE: My newspaper was torn.

PRONOUN: Mine was torn.

Apply what you have learned so far by doing Exercise 4 for Subskill 6A.

Exercise 4 for Subskill 6A

Circle all the adjectives in the sentences on page 122. Draw an arrow to the noun each adjective modifies. Some sentences may not contain any adjectives.

EXAMPLE: (Neither) girl could find (her) homework.

1. I tried on every dress in my closet.

2. Some people lost their tempers.

3. Neither fit me.

4. His girlfriend gave him another chance.

5. Both are going out tonight.

Check your answers on page 25 in the Answer Key for Book Two. Then review pages 115–121. When you think you understand all the different kinds of words that can be adjectives, do the following exercise, which is a summary review of this subskill.

Exercise 5 for Subskill 6A

In this exercise, remember that the part of speech of a word is determined by how the word is used in a sentence.

- Underline the verbs twice.
- Underline the nouns once.
- Circle all the adjectives.

Review your work to be sure you have completed each step.

EXAMPLE: The (old) woman was lending (her) friends (some) money.

1. The corner store sells fresh bread, ice-cold drinks, canned fruits and vegetables, and camping supplies.

2. Piercing screams filled the air.

3. The worried man had discovered a frightening secret.

4. Those American soldiers have won three medals.

5. Our bank statement contained several mistakes.

6. He was heating some frozen vegetables in an aluminum pan.

7. The mysterious visitor had a French accent.

8. This old coat needs a few new buttons.

9. Each girl took her turn.

10. The lost child was crying.

Check your answers on page 25 in the Answer Key for Book Two. If you correctly answered all 10 items, go to Subskill 6B. If not, do the Supplemental Exercise for Subskill 6A.

Supplemental Exercise for Subskill 6A

Review the information about adjectives on pages 115–121. Then do the following exercise.

Read sentences 1–10 and do the following:

- Underline each noun once.
- Underline each verb twice.
- Circle each adjective.

Review your work to be sure you have completed each step.

EXAMPLE: The (frightened) witness presented (some) (interesting) evidence.

1. I will mend your torn jeans.

2. The defeated American team did not win a gold medal.

3. That store sells imported straw baskets.

4. My best friend always orders fried rice in Chinese restaurants.

5. Both men wanted another chance.

6. Neither had done his best work the first time.

7. That young woman is running around the park.

8. She owns those blue running shoes.

9. The Americans and the Canadians discussed farming methods.

10. Rose likes Canadian bacon.

Check your answers on page 26 in the Answer Key for Book Two. If you correctly answered 8 of 10 items, go to Subskill 6B. If not, ask your instructor for help.

Subskill 6B: Locating Adjectives by Their Position in the Sentence

When you complete this subskill, you will be able to identify adjectives that are used in different parts of a sentence. You will be able to recognize adjectives that come right before and right after a noun. You will be able to recognize adjectives that modify the subject but are located in the predicate.

Most Adjectives Come Right Before Nouns

As you recall from the previous subskill, most adjectives come before the nouns they modify.

George bought a <u>secondhand</u> car.

<u>Secondhand</u> modifies <u>car</u>.

REMEMBER: More than one adjective can modify a single noun.

George bought a <u>cheap</u> <u>secondhand</u> car.

Some Adjectives Come Right After Nouns

Occasionally adjectives are placed after the nouns they modify. Usually, this placement is for emphasis. Examine the sentence below.

          Adj   Adj
The weather, cold and rainy, caused many fans to stay home.

<u>Cold</u> and <u>rainy</u> modify <u>weather</u>.

Predicate Adjectives Come After Linking Verbs

A predicate adjective is an adjective in the predicate that modifies the subject. Predicate adjectives occur only in sentences that have linking verbs (<u>be</u>, <u>am</u>, <u>is</u>, <u>are</u>, <u>was</u>, <u>were</u>, <u>look</u>, <u>feel</u>, <u>taste</u>, <u>appear</u>, <u>become</u>, etc.). The predicate adjective usually comes right after the linking verb.

        S   LV   PA
My mother became ill last spring.

<u>Ill</u> follows the linking verb <u>become</u> and modifies the simple subject <u>mother</u>. <u>Ill</u> is a predicate adjective.

The subject may be modified by more than one predicate adjective.

S   LV   PA   PA
The old man's smile was crooked and frightening.

Crooked and frightening are predicate adjectives because they follow the linking verb was and describe the simple subject smile.

Predicate adjectives can modify pronouns as well as nouns. An adjective following a linking verb modifies the subject of the sentence. It doesn't matter whether that subject is a noun or a pronoun.

S   LV   PA   PA
She seems lazy and inconsiderate.

Lazy and inconsiderate are predicate adjectives because they follow the linking verb seems and describe the simple subject she, which is a pronoun.

Predicate Adjective or Verb?

You have learned that present participles (-ing words) and past participles (which usually end in -ed) can be used as verbs. You have also learned that these parts can be used as adjectives. Notice how the -ing word encouraging is used in the following sentences.

V
Jeff is encouraging us.

Encouraging is the main verb in an action verb phrase. It tells what Jeff is doing.

Adj
We appreciated your encouraging words.

Encouraging is not the verb in this sentence. It is an adjective used to describe the noun words.

When -ing words are used as predicate adjectives, it can be difficult to distinguish them from verbs. Can you tell how the word encouraging is used differently in the following two sentences?

S   V
They were encouraging you.

S   V   PA
Their advice was encouraging.

In the first sentence, encouraging is an action verb. It tells what they were doing. In the second sentence, encouraging is not an action verb. It is a predicate adjective that follows the linking verb was. In this sentence, encouraging does not tell what someone was doing. Instead, it describes the subject advice.

Now see if you can follow the uses of the past participles frozen and bored in the sentences on the following page.

S   V   Adj
We stocked the freezer with frozen vegetables.

<u>Frozen</u> is an adjective describing the noun <u>vegetables</u>.

S   LV   PA
The vegetables are frozen.

<u>Frozen</u> is a predicate adjective that follows the linking verb <u>are</u> and describes the subject <u>vegetables</u>.

S   V
The vegetables have frozen.

<u>Have frozen</u> is an action verb phrase. The words <u>have frozen</u> tell what happened. They express an action that took place.

S   V
The speaker bored us.

<u>Bored</u> is an action verb. It tells what the speaker did.

S   LV   PA
We are bored with this meeting.

In this sentence, <u>bored</u> is a predicate adjective following the linking verb <u>are</u> and describing the subject <u>we</u>.

Apply what you have learned about locating adjectives in sentences by doing the following exercise.

Exercise for Subskill 6B

Read each of the sentences below carefully. Then do the following:

· Underline each verb twice.
· Underline the nouns and pronouns once.
· Circle all adjectives.
· Label predicate adjectives <u>PA</u>.

Review your work to be sure that you have done each step.

EXAMPLES: The (tired)(old) man sat under the (shady)(oak) tree.
                          PA   PA
He was hungry and penniless.

1. He is hard-working and responsible.

2. Early German settlers built this old farmhouse.

3. Six exhausted runners, panting for breath, crossed the finish line.

4. Susan is planning an Easter vacation to the national park.

5. She will need adequate camping gear, a state road map, non-perishable foods, and first aid supplies.

6. My cousin is helping me with a difficult problem.

7. We were excited about the good news.

8. That exciting movie has thrilled many people.

9. My friends are understanding and supportive.

10. The weather, clear and balmy, was perfect for our family reunion.

Check your answers on page 26 in the Answer Key for Book Two. If you correctly answered all 10 items, go to Subskill 6C. If not, do the Supplemental Exercise for Subskill 6B.

Supplemental Exercise for Subskill 6B

Review the information about locating adjectives on pages 124–126. Then do the following exercise.

Read each of the sentences below carefully. Then do the following:

- Underline each verb twice.
- Underline the nouns and pronouns once.
- Circle all adjectives.
- Label predicate adjectives PA.

Review your work to be sure that you have completed each step.

EXAMPLE: Ralph, (tired) but (happy) arrived at (our) house.

1. We are working on an interesting assignment.

2. I live in that large brick building.

3. My apartment is small and cozy.

4. The kitchen sink is broken.

5. The commuter train, crowded and noisy, pulled into the station.

6. That river is polluted.

7.   Steve watches the late evening news every night.

8.   The unemployed man, confident and hopeful, was looking for work.

9.   That new mystery movie is boring.

10.   We have just eaten a new frozen dessert.

Check your answers on pages 26 and 27 in the Answer Key for Book Two. If you correctly answered 8 of 10 items, go to Subskill 6C. If not, ask your instructor for help.

Subskill 6C: Recognizing Adjectives by Their Endings

When you complete this subskill, you will be able to recognize adjectives that have special adjective endings. You will also be able to form adjectives by adding the special endings to words that are not adjectives.

Identifying Special Adjective Endings

So far you have learned to recognize adjectives by their function. (They answer "What kind?", "Which one?", or "How many?" about nouns and pronouns.) You have learned to locate adjectives by their position in a sentence. (They may come before or after the nouns they modify, or they may follow a linking verb.)

A third way to recognize some adjectives is by their **suffixes, or word endings.** Words ending in the suffixes -ic, -able, -ible, -ous, -ious, -itious, -less, -al, -ive, -ative and -ful are usually adjectives.

The dinner was delicious.

He was an amiable salesman.

Not all adjectives have special adjective endings. However, knowing the endings may help you identify some adjectives.

If you cannot recognize an adjective by its function or placement, look for an adjective suffix.

Suffix	Meaning	Example
-able (-ible)	capable of being or causing	comfortable terrible
-ic	having the character or form of	panoramic alcoholic

Suffix	Meaning	Example
-ous (-ious, -itious)	full of, possessing qualities of	ridicul<u>ous</u> fict<u>itious</u>
-less	without	use<u>less</u> help<u>less</u> hope<u>less</u>
-al	related to or characterized by	nation<u>al</u> recreation<u>al</u>
-ive (-ative)	performing or tending toward an action	talk<u>ative</u> discurs<u>ive</u>
-ful	full, filled with	beauti<u>ful</u> joy<u>ful</u>

Forming Adjectives by Adding Adjective Endings

You can change some words from one part of speech to another by adding the right endings. You can often form an adjective from a noun or verb or other part of speech. Notice how the following adjectives have been formed from other parts of speech by the addition of adjective endings.

child<u>ish</u> = child (noun) + ish

wonder<u>ful</u> = wonder (noun) + ful

agree<u>able</u> = agree (verb) + able

Sometimes you have to change the base word slightly before you add an adjective ending.

beauty + ful = beaut<u>iful</u>
Change <u>y</u> preceded by consonant to <u>i</u> before adding ending.

fame + ous = fam<u>ous</u>
Drop silent <u>-e</u> before an ending that starts with vowel.

ambition + ous = ambit<u>ious</u>
Drop the noun ending <u>-ion</u> before adding adjective ending <u>-ious</u>.

When you are not sure how to spell an adjective with a special ending, look up the word in the dictionary.

Apply what you have learned about adjective endings by doing the following exercise.

Exercise for Subskill 6C

For each item below, do the following:

- Write the adjective that can be formed from each combination.

- Write a sentence using each adjective.

- Circle the adjective and draw an arrow to the noun it modifies.

Review your work to be sure you have completed each step. Use your dictionary to check spellings and meanings if necessary.

EXAMPLE: care + less = _____careless_____

His actions were (careless)

1. profession + al = _____

_____

2. defense + ive = _____

_____

3. pity + ful = _____

_____

4. space + ious = _____

_____

5. atom + ic = _____

_____

Have your instructor check your work. If you correctly answered all 5 items, go to Subskill 6D. If not, do the Supplemental Exercise for Subskill 6C.

Supplemental Exercise for Subskill 6C

Review the information about adjective endings on pages 128 and 129. Then do the following for each item below:

- Write the adjective that can be formed from each combination.

- Write a sentence using each adjective.

- Circle the adjective and draw an arrow to the noun it modifies.

Review your work to be sure you have completed each step. Use your dictionary to check spellings and meanings if necessary.

EXAMPLE: angel + ic = ___angelic___

___The child had an (angelic) smile.___

1. response + ible = _____

   _____

2. success + ful = _____

   _____

3. nature + al = _____

   _____

4. enjoy + able = _____

   _____

5. study + ous = _____

   _____

Have your instructor check your work. If you correctly answered 4 of 5 items, go to Subskill 6D. If not, ask your instructor for help.

Subskill 6D: Using Adjectives to Make Comparisons

When you complete this subskill, you will be able to use the comparative and superlative forms of adjectives correctly.

Making Comparisons with Adjectives

Most adjectives have three forms: the **positive**, the **comparative**, and the **superlative**.
   The positive form is used when no comparison is being made.

Joe is <u>tall</u>.

The comparative form is used to compare two items.

Joe is <u>taller</u> than Ray.

The superlative form is used to compare more than two items.

Joe is the <u>tallest</u> man on the team.

Making Comparisons Using -er and -est

For one-syllable adjectives and for two-syllable adjectives that end in -y, add -er to form the comparative and -est to form the superlative. Study the following chart to help you add -er and -est.

Rule	Positive (Base Form)	Comparative (used to compare two items)	Superlative (used to compare three or more items)
If an adjective already ends with the letter -e, just add -r or -st.	nice fine	nicer finer	the nicest the finest
If a one-syllable adjective ends in a single vowel followed by a single consonant, double the final consonant and add -er or -est.	thin hot flat	thinner hotter flatter	the thinnest the hottest the flattest
If adjectives end in -y, change y to i and then add -er and -est.	happy early funny	happier earlier funnier	the happiest the earliest the funniest

Making Comparisons with More, Most, Less, and Least

Most two-syllable adjectives and all adjectives of more than two syllables use the words more or less to compare two items. The words the most or the least are used to compare three or more items. Study the following chart.

Number of Syllables	Positive	Comparative (used to compare two items)	Superlative (used to compare three or more items)
2	noisy frosty	noisier frostier	the noisiest the frostiest
2	recent pleasing	more recent less pleasing	the most recent the least pleasing
3	successful beautiful	more successful less beautiful	the most successful the least beautiful

Look at the two- and three-syllable words in this chart, and you can see why it would be awkward to add -er and -est to most of them. It would be difficult to pronounce words such as successfuler, success-fulest, beautifuler, and beautifulest. Therefore, words like these are not used. Instead, more or less is added to most words with two or more syllables to form the comparative, and the most or the least is added to form the superlative.

Making Comparisons with Irregular Adjectives

Some adjectives have comparative and superlative forms that are very different from the positive (the base form). These adjectives are called **irregular adjectives.** Study the following chart of irregular adjectives.

Positive (Base Form)	Comparative (two or more)	Superlative (three or more)
good	better	the best
well (meaning "not sick")	better	the best
bad	worse	the worst
many	more	the most
much	more	the most
little (meaning "small in amount or degree")*	less	the least

*When little is used to mean "small in size," its comparative form is littler and its superlative form is littlest.

Avoid Double Comparisons

Never use both -er and more or both -est and most in a comparison.

DON'T SAY: The rules are more stricter here.

SAY: The rules are stricter here.

DON'T SAY: That is the most beautifulest sunset I've ever seen!

SAY: That is the most beautiful sunset I've ever seen.

Don't use more or most with the comparative or superlative forms of irregular adjectives either. Don't add -er or -est to an irregular comparative or superlative form.

DON'T SAY: She plays more better than I do.

SAY: She plays better than I do.

DON'T SAY: The final score was more worse than I expected.

DON'T SAY: The score was worser than I expected.

SAY: The score was <u>worse</u> than I expected.

Apply what you have learned about comparative and superlative forms of adjectives by doing the following exercise.

Exercise for Subskill 6D

Fill in the blanks with the comparative and superlative forms of the adjectives given.

EXAMPLE: much   (a)   They have <u>more</u> plants in their apartment than their neighbors do.

  (b)   They have the <u>most</u> plants of anyone in the neighborhood.

1. pretty   (a)   The blue dress is _____ than the white one.

  (b)   That dress is the _____ of the three.

2. strict   (a)   My parents were _____ than yours.

  (b)   My parents were the _____ in the community.

3. young   (a)   Frank is the _____ of the two boys.

  (b)   Frank is the _____ of the five sons.

4. warm   (a)   It is _____ today than it was yesterday.

  (b)   Today is the _____ day of the summer.

5. appealing   (a)   This picture is _____ than the other.

  (b)   This picture is the _____ one in the whole museum.

6. bad   (a)   My headache is _____ today than it was yesterday.

(b) This is the _____ headache I've had all week.

7. little   (a) He has _____ money than Melvin.

            (b) He has the _____ money of any of his friends.

8. unusual   (a) Her idea was _____ than mine.

            (b) It was the _____ idea I've ever heard.

9. curly   (a) Her hair is _____ than her sister's.

            (b) Their father has the _____ hair in the family.

10. hot   (a) It is _____ this week than it was last week.

            (b) August was the _____ month of all.

Check your answers on page 27 in the Answer Key for Book Two. If you correctly answered all 10 items, go to Self-Check on page 136. If not, do the Supplemental Exercise for Subskill 6D.

Supplemental Exercise for Subskill 6D

Part A. Complete the chart below. Be sure your spelling is correct.

	Positive	Comparative	Superlative
EXAMPLE:	much	more	the most
1.	attractive		
2.	neat		
3.	big		
4.	talkative		
5.	friendly		
6.	little		
7.	bad		

	Positive	Comparative	Superlative
8.	good		
9.	easy		
10.	many		

Part B. Write your own sentence using the forms of the adjectives indicated.

EXAMPLE: many — comparing two

She has more friends than I do.

11. good — comparing three or more   (superlative form)

_____

12. original — comparing two   (comparative form)

_____

13. lovely — comparing two   (comparative form)

_____

14. little — comparing three or more (superlative form)

_____

15. hot — comparing two (comparative form)

_____

Check Part A on page 27 in the Answer Key for Book Two. Ask your instructor to check your original sentences. If you correctly completed 12 of 15 items, go to the Self-Check. If not, ask your instructor for help.

SELF–CHECK: SKILL UNIT 6

Part A. Circle all the adjectives in the following sentences.

EXAMPLE: I saw (three) (interesting) movies.

1. Those wool sweaters are expensive.

2. A spectacular sunset, red and orange, filled the evening sky.

3. The howling winds swayed the fragile young trees.

4. Three French diplomats met with the frightened American citizens.

5. Plastic bottles are lighter than glass bottles.

6. Each woman explained her answer.

7. That newspaper article is fascinating but unbelievable.

8. Both seemed interested in my reaction.

9. I am showing two new employees the cafeteria.

10. Our trip was delightful and affordable.

Part B. Each of the following sentences contains an incorrect adjective. Underline the incorrect word. Then rewrite each sentence correctly.

EXAMPLE: Your answer was <u>more</u> better than mine.

_____Your answer was better than mine._____

11. Them books are not yours.

    _____

12. Your picture is more prettier than his.

    _____

13. That there supermarket is always crowded.

    _____

14. Al is the oldest of the two brothers.

    _____

15. This chair is comfortabler than the sofa.

    _____

16. That is the worse song I have ever heard.

    _____

Check your answers on page 28 in the Answer Key for Book Two. If you correctly answered 12 of 16 items, you have mastered these skills. If not, ask your instructor for help.

Skill Unit 7
IDENTIFYING ADVERBS
AND USING THEM CORRECTLY

What Skills You Need to Begin: You need to be able to identify nouns (Skill Unit 1), verbs (Skill Units 3 and 4), and adjectives (Skill Unit 6).

What Skills You Will Learn: After completing this skill unit, you will be able to identify all kinds of adverbs and use them correctly. You will be able to form adverbs by adding ly to adjectives. You will be able to write the comparative and superlative forms of adverbs and use these forms correctly. You will be able to choose the proper adjective or adverb form required in a sentence and avoid common adverb usage problems.

Why You Need These Skills: In Skill Unit 6 you learned that adjectives can make language more informative and interesting by telling "what kind," "how many," or "which one." In this skill unit you will learn how adverbs add to the meaning of a sentence by telling "how," "when," "how often," "where," or "to what extent." By using adverbs carefully, you can communicate more precisely and effectively.

How You Will Show What You Have Learned: You will take the Self-Check at the end of this unit on page 158. The Self-Check contains 10 items. If you answer 8 of 10 items correctly, you will have shown that you have mastered these skills.

If you feel that you have already mastered these skills, turn to the end of this unit and complete the Self-Check on page 158.

Subskill 7A: Identifying Adverbs

When you complete this subskill, you will be able to identify adverbs by the questions they answer about action verbs, adjectives, and other adverbs.

Like adjectives, **adverbs** are modifiers. They add to or change the meaning of other words in the sentence. In Skill Unit 6, you learned how adjectives modify nouns and pronouns. In this unit, you will learn how adverbs modify verbs, adjectives, or other adverbs.

Adverbs Usually Modify Action Verbs

Most adverbs modify action verbs. They tell <u>how</u>, <u>where</u>, <u>when</u>, or <u>how often</u> an action is done. One good way to find adverbs is to look for an action verb and then ask yourself if there are any words in the sentence that answer the questions "How?", "Where?", "When?", or "How often?" about that action.

Some Adverbs Answer the Question "How?"

We met <u>secretly</u>.

<u>Met</u> is an action verb. <u>Secretly</u> modifies <u>met</u>. How did we meet? <u>Secretly</u>. <u>Secretly</u> is an adverb modifying the action verb <u>met</u>.

I drive <u>carefully</u>.

<u>Drive</u> is an action verb. How do I drive? <u>Carefully</u>. <u>Carefully</u> is an adverb modifying the action verb <u>drive</u>.

The men ate <u>quickly</u>.

<u>Ate</u> is an action verb. How did the men eat? <u>Quickly</u>. <u>Quickly</u> is an adverb modifying the action verb <u>ate</u>.

The boss shouted <u>angrily</u>.

<u>Shouted</u> is an action verb. How did the boss shout? <u>Angrily</u>. <u>Angrily</u> is an adverb modifying the action verb <u>shouted</u>.

John and his partner play ball <u>alike</u>.

<u>Play</u> is an action verb. How do John and his partner play? <u>Alike</u>. <u>Alike</u> is an adverb modifying the action verb <u>play</u>.

Some Adverbs Answer the Question "When?"

My brother <u>recently</u> moved to Atlanta.

<u>Moved</u> is an action verb. When did my brother move? <u>Recently</u>. <u>Recently</u> is an adverb modifying the action verb <u>move</u>.

The movie will start <u>soon</u>.

<u>Will start</u> is an action verb phrase. When will the movie start? <u>Soon</u>. <u>Soon</u> is an adverb modifying the action verb phrase <u>will start</u>.

Are you leaving <u>now</u>?

<u>Are leaving</u> is an action verb phrase. When are you leaving? <u>Now</u>. <u>Now</u> is an adverb modifying the action verb phrase <u>are leaving</u>.

Some Adverbs Answer the Question "How Often?" or "How Many Times?"

I <u>always</u> brush my teeth.

<u>Brush</u> is an action verb. How often do I brush? Always. <u>Always</u> is an adverb modifying the action verb <u>brush</u>.

He <u>never</u> lies.

<u>Lies</u> is an action verb, used here to mean "not telling the truth." How often does he lie? Never. <u>Never</u> is an adverb modifying the action verb <u>lies</u>.

I <u>seldom</u> exercise.

<u>Exercise</u> is an action verb. How often do I exercise? Seldom. <u>Seldom</u> is an adverb modifying the action verb <u>exercise</u>.

I have seen that movie <u>twice</u>.

<u>Have seen</u> is an action verb phrase. How many times did I see the movie? Twice. <u>Twice</u> is an adverb modifying the action verb phrase <u>have seen</u>.

Some Adverbs Answer the Question "Where?"

The Smiths live <u>here</u>.

<u>Live</u> is an action verb. Where do the Smiths live? Here. <u>Here</u> is an adverb modifying the action verb <u>live</u>.

The troops moved <u>forward</u>.

<u>Moved</u> is an action verb. Where did the troops move? Forward. <u>Forward</u> is an adverb modifying the action verb <u>moved</u>.

The young girl ran <u>away</u>.

<u>Ran</u> is an action verb. Where did the girl run? Away. <u>Away</u> is an adverb modifying the action verb <u>ran</u>.

Adverbs Also Modify Adjectives and Other Adverbs

Not all adverbs modify action verbs. Some adverbs modify adjectives and even other adverbs. These adverbs answer the question "How?", meaning "To what extent?"

His child is <u>rather</u> shy.

<u>Shy</u> is a predicate adjective because it follows the linking verb <u>is</u> and modifies the simple subject <u>child</u>. How shy? Rather shy. <u>Rather</u> is an adverb modifying the predicate adjective <u>shy</u>.

Frank skis <u>extremely</u> well.

<u>Well</u> is an adverb because it tells how Frank <u>skis</u>. How well? Extremely well. <u>Extremely</u> is an adverb modifying the adverb <u>well</u>.

You are <u>too</u> impatient.

<u>Impatient</u> is a predicate adjective modifying the subject <u>you</u>. How impatient? Too impatient. <u>Too</u> is an adverb modifying the predicate adjective <u>impatient</u>.

That story is <u>more</u> interesting than the other.

<u>Interesting</u> is a predicate adjective modifying the subject <u>story</u>. How interesting? More interesting. <u>More</u> is an adverb modifying the predicate adjective <u>interesting</u>.

Other adverbs that modify adjectives and other adverbs include <u>very</u>, <u>almost</u>, <u>extremely</u>, <u>less</u>, <u>quite</u>, <u>rather</u>, and <u>somewhat</u>.
A sentence may contain several adverbs.

That sprinter <u>always</u> runs <u>quite</u> <u>fast</u>.

How does he run? <u>Fast</u>. How fast? <u>Quite</u> fast. How often does he run quite fast? <u>Always</u>. <u>Always</u>, <u>quite</u>, and <u>fast</u> are adverbs.

Some words that are usually nouns may do the work of adverbs.

I went <u>home</u>.

The action verb is <u>went</u>. Where did I go? Home. <u>Home</u>, usually a noun, is an adverb in this sentence.

Apply what you have learned about adverbs by doing the following exercise.

Exercise for Subskill 7A

Look at the underlined adverb in each sentence. Draw an arrow to the word each underlined adverb modifies. If the adverb modifies an action verb, write "How?, When?, How often? or Where?" in the blank to show what question the adverb answers about the verb. If the adverb modifies an adjective or another adverb, write "How?" (meaning "To what extent?") in the blank to show what question the adverb answers.

EXAMPLE: The dog barked <u>loudly</u>.   ___barked how?___

1. She is <u>extremely</u> unhappy. _____

2. We will begin the project <u>immediately</u>. _____

3. He left his coat <u>downstairs</u>. _____

4. The child giggled <u>constantly</u>. _____

5. Jan is leaving town <u>today</u>. _____

6. We were working <u>busily</u> in the kitchen. _____

7. <u>Sometimes</u> I enjoy a midnight movie. _____

8. Those shoes are <u>too</u> small for your feet. _____

9. During winter months people must dress <u>warmly</u>. _____

10. She smiled <u>sweetly</u>, spoke <u>softly</u>, and <u>gently</u> patted the child's hand. _____

Check your answers on pages 28 and 29 in the Answer Key for Book Two. If you correctly answered all 10 items, go to Subskill 7B. If not, do the Supplemental Exercise for Subskill 7A.

Supplemental Exercise for Subskill 7A

Review the information about questions adverbs answer on pages 138–141. Then do the following exercise.

Look at the underlined adverb in each sentence. Draw an arrow to the word each underlined adverb modifies. Then, in the blank, write the question the adverb answers.

EXAMPLE: Alice runs <u>quite</u> fast.   <u>how fast?</u> _____

1. The picnic was planned very <u>carefully</u>.

   _____

2. Anne always talks <u>too</u> slowly.

   _____

3. The crowd was talking <u>excitedly.</u>

   _____

4. She <u>frequently</u> visits us. _____

5. <u>Soon</u> their mother will prepare hot chocolate.

   _____

6. He drove <u>home</u> recklessly. _____

7. Can you read this label <u>easily</u>?

   _____

8. She completed her work <u>quickly</u>.

   _____

9. The bag was <u>almost</u> empty. _____

10. I'll call you <u>tomorrow</u>. _____

Check your answers on page 29 in the Answer Key for Book Two. If you correctly answered 8 of 10 sentences, go to Subskill 7B. If not, ask your instructor for help.

Subskill 7B: Positioning Adverbs in a Sentence

When you complete this subskill, you will be able to identify adverbs that appear in different positions in a sentence. You will be able to position adverbs carefully in a sentence so that you say exactly what you mean.

Some adverbs can appear almost anywhere in a sentence. Often the position of the adverb does not affect the meaning of the sentence.

Silently the burglar crept through the house.

The burglar silently crept through the house.

The burglar crept silently through the house.

The burglar crept through the house silently.

Sometimes, though, changing the position of the adverb can change the meaning of a sentence.

First, he arrived at the party. (That was the first thing he did. Then he did something else.)

He arrived first at the party. (No one else arrived before him.)

You never told me to call. (You didn't say anything about it.)

You told me never to call. (You specifically told me not to call.)

Adverbs that modify adjectives or other adverbs come right before the words they modify.

Artie is very sad.

The time passed too slowly.

Apply what you have learned about positioning adverbs by doing the following exercise.

Exercise for Subskill 7B

Expand the following sentences by using the adverbs given in parentheses. In some sentences the adverb must be placed in a specific position to make the meaning clear. In other sentences, you have a choice of where to put the adverb.

EXAMPLE: We ate our food. (slowly)

          We slowly ate our food.

OR: Slowly we ate our food.

OR: We ate our food slowly.

1.   The boy looked for his dog. (frantically)

_____

2.   He crossed the finish line. (first) (Make it clear that he was the winner.)

_____

3.   The puppy whined outside the door. (sadly)

_____

4.   She told me to tell a lie. (never) (She told me not to lie.)

_____

5.   She told me to tell a lie. (never) (She didn't tell me to lie.)

_____

Check your answers on page 29 in the Answer Key for Book Two. If you correctly wrote all 5 sentences, go Subskill 7C. If not, do the Supplemental Exercise for Subskill 7B.

Supplemental Exercise for Subskill 7B

Review the information about positioning adverbs on page 143. Then do the following exercise.

Expand these basic sentences by using the adverbs given in parentheses. In some sentences, the adverbs must be placed in a specific position to make the meaning clear. In other sentences, you have a choice of where to put the adverb.

EXAMPLE: His hair is short. (very) (Make it clear that his hair is shorter than usual.)

        His hair is very short.

1.   She asked me to trust her. (always) (Make it clear that she asked me all the time.)

_____

2. She asked me to trust her. (always) (Make it clear that she wanted me to trust her forever.)

_____

3. I lost all of my money. (almost) (Make it clear that I could have lost my money, but I didn't.)

_____

4. I lost all of my money. (almost) (Make it clear that I lost most of my money, but not all of it.)

_____

5. The sun came out. (suddenly)

_____

Check your answers on page 29 in the Answer Key for Book Two. If you correctly wrote 4 of 5 sentences, go to Subskill 7C. If not, ask your instructor for help.

Subskill 7C: Forming Adverbs from Adjectives

When you complete this subskill, you will know how to change adjectives to adverbs by adding -ly.

Adding ly to Form Adverbs

Many adverbs are formed by adding ly to an adjective.

ADJECTIVES:

The cloth is soft.

The syrup was sweet.

ADVERBS:

She spoke softly.

The child smiled sweetly.

Follow these rules for adding ly to form adverbs:

Rule 1:   To change most adjectives to adverbs, simply add -ly.

sudden + ly = suddenly

The car made a sudden stop.

The car stopped suddenly.

Rule 2:   For adjectives that end in -le, drop the e and then add y.

> The shoes were comfortable.   (adjective)
>
> The shoes fit comfortably.   (adverb)

Rule 3:   For adjectives that end in ll, simply add y.

> The apartment was full of people.   (adjective)
>
> The apartment was fully furnished.   (adverb)

Rule 4:   For adjectives that end in y, change the y to i and add ly.

> We were busy.   (adjective)
>
> We were working busily.   (adverb)

Rule 5:   For adjectives that end in ic, add ally.

> The story had a tragic ending.   (adjective)
>
> The story ended tragically.   (adverb)

Rule 6:   Some adjectives that end in ly remain the same when they are used as adverbs.

> We took the early train.   (adjective)
>
> The train arrived early.   (adverb)
>
> We buy the daily newspaper.   (adjective)
>
> We buy it daily.   (adverb)

Rule 7:   Some adjectives that end in ly do not have an adverb form. They can only be used as adjectives.

> ADJECTIVES: friendly, lovely, lonely, lively

Rule 8:   Some adjectives that do not end in -ly remain the same when they are used as adverbs.

> ADVERBS OR ADJECTIVES: high, low, fast, straight, long, late
>
> We travelled on a fast train.
>
> The train went fast.

Rule 9:   For adjectives that end in al, you add ly. Often, however, the al in the adverb form is not pronounced, so many people leave it out. You must remember that the adverb was formed from an adjective that ended in al in order to spell the adverb correctly. Memorize these forms.

ADJECTIVES: accidental   incidental   magical   typical   musical

ADVERBS: accidentally incidentally magically typically musically

Rule 10: Some adverb forms have to be memorized.

ADJECTIVES:	whole	true
ADVERBS:	wholly	truly

Apply what you have learned about changing adjectives to adverbs by doing the following exercise.

Exercise for Subskill 7C

Look at the following pairs of sentences. The first sentence in each pair contains an adjective that is underlined. The second sentence in each pair contains a blank space. Fill in the blank with the adverb form of each adjective.

EXAMPLE: The shooting was underline{accidental}.

The shooting occurred ____accidentally._____

1. She is a careful writer.

    She writes _____.

2. The children were noisy.

    The children played _____.

3. Her uneasiness was noticeable.

    She was _____ uneasy.

4. They did sloppy work.

    Their work was _____ done.

5. This is a fantastic product.

    It works _____.

6. We went to an early show.

    It started _____.

7. The bird had a shrill call.

    It called _____ to its mate.

8. We were driving on a <u>straight</u> road.

   We drove _____ down the road.

9. His answer was <u>typical</u>.

   He answered _____.

10. This story is <u>true</u>.

    This story is _____ wonderful.

Check your answers on page 29 in the Answer Key for Book Two. If you correctly answered all 10 sentences, go to Subskill 7D. If not, do the Supplemental Exercise for Subskill 7C.

Supplemental Exercise for Subskill 7C

Review the information about changing adjectives to adverbs on pages 145–147. Then do the following exercise.

The first sentence in each pair contains an adjective that has been underlined. The second sentence in each pair contains a blank. Fill in the blank with the adverb form of each adjective.

EXAMPLE: They seemed <u>happy</u>.

           They seemed ___<u>happily</u>___ married.

1. The <u>basic</u> idea was unchanged.

   The idea was _____ unchanged.

2. We were <u>hungry</u>.

   We ate _____.

3. The <u>whole</u> project was completed.

   The project was _____ completed.

4. They made their <u>final</u> offer.

   They _____ made an offer.

5. The <u>gentle</u> veterinarian lifted the cat.

   The veterinarian _____ lifted the cat.

6. She takes a <u>daily</u> vitamin.

   She takes vitamins _____.

7. The prices were <u>reasonable</u>.

The items were _____ priced.

8. We need a <u>fast</u> reply.

They replied _____.

9. Jan was <u>grateful</u> for our help.

She smiled at us _____.

10. Roberto gave us a <u>full</u> report.

We _____ agreed with his conclusions.

Check your answers on pages 29 and 30 in the Answer Key for Book Two. If you correctly wrote 8 of 10 adverbs, go to Subskill 7D. If not, ask your instructor for help.

Subskill 7D: Using Adverbs to Make Comparisons

When you complete this subskill, you will be able to use the comparative and superlative forms of adverbs correctly.

Making Comparisons with Adverbs

In Skill Unit 6, you learned that most adjectives have three forms—the positive, the comparative, and the superlative. You learned that the comparative and superlative forms are used to make comparisons. Most **adverbs** may be used to make comparisons too. They too have positive, comparative, and superlative forms.

The **positive** form is used when no comparison is being made.

Al eats slowly.

I arrived early.

The comparative form is used to compare two items.

Kim eats more slowly than Al.

I arrived earlier than you did.

The **superlative** form is used to compare more than two items.

Of all the members of my family, Sylvia eats the most slowly.

Of all the guests at the party, I arrived the earliest.

Use the following rules to make comparisons with adverbs.

Rule 1: For one-syllable adverbs, add <u>er</u> to form the comparative and <u>est</u> to form the superlative.

Jane worked <u>hard</u>.

Stu worked <u>harder</u> than Jane.

Of all the employees, Linda worked the <u>hardest</u>.

Rule 2: For adverbs of more than one syllable, use <u>more</u> to form the comparative and <u>most</u> to form the superlative.

I often win the game.

She wins <u>more</u> often than I do.

He wins the <u>most</u> often.

Rick took my complaint seriously.

Loretta took my complaint <u>more</u> seriously than Rick did.

Of all my friends, Angela took my complaint the <u>most</u> seriously.

EXCEPTION: To form the comparative and superlative forms of the adverb <u>early</u>, add <u>er</u> and <u>est</u>: early, earlier, earliest.

Rule 3: The adverbs <u>well</u> and <u>badly</u> have irregular comparative and superlative forms.

POSITIVE: well badly
COMPARATIVE: better worse
SUPERLATIVE: the best the worst

I play <u>well</u>.

She plays <u>better</u> than I do.

You play the <u>best</u>.

Our team played <u>badly</u>.

Their team played <u>worse</u> than ours.

Of all the teams in the playoff, theirs played the <u>worst</u>.

Rule 4: Many adverbs have no comparative or superlative forms. These include the adverbs that tell "where" (<u>outside</u>, <u>here</u>), some adverbs that tell "when" (<u>always</u>, <u>never</u>), and many adverbs that modify adjectives and other adverbs (<u>too</u>, <u>quite</u>, <u>very</u>, etc.).

Rule 5: Remember to use the comparative, not the superlative, to compare two items.

DON'T SAY: Of the two brothers, Tom drives the fastest.
SAY: Of the two brothers, Tom drives <u>faster</u>.

DON'T SAY: Of the two brothers, Tom runs the most quickly.
SAY: Of the two brothers, Tom runs <u>more</u> quickly.

Rule 6: Remember not to use two comparative forms.

DON'T SAY: He visits more oftener than I do.
SAY: He visits <u>more often</u> than I do.

DON'T SAY: They arrived more sooner than I expected.
SAY: They arrived <u>sooner</u> than I expected.

Apply what you have learned about using adverbs to make comparisons by doing the following exercise.

Exercise for Subskill 7D

Fill in the blanks with the comparative and superlative forms of each adverb given.

EXAMPLE: quickly José works <u>more quickly</u> than Pat.
José works the <u>most</u> quickly of all.

1. recently I started working here _____ than you did.
Of the three of us, Helen started working here

_____ .

2. close Sheila was sitting _____ to the door than I was.
Of all the people in the room, Frank was sitting

_____ to the door.

3. often I go there _____ than she does.
Of the three of us, Ralph goes there

_____ .

4. well Mary sings _____ than Stella.

Of the three women, Angela sings _____ .

5. early We left _____ than you did.

Of all the guests, we left _____ .

Check your answers on page 30 in the Answer Key for Book Two. If you correctly answered all 5 items, go to Subskill 7E. If not, do the Supplemental Exercise for Subskill 7D.

Supplemental Exercise for Subskill 7D

Review the information about forming the comparative and superlative forms of adverbs on pages 149–151. Then do the following exercise.

Fill in the blanks with the comparative and superlative forms of the adverbs given.

EXAMPLE: seriously   Today's article treats the problems <u>more seriously</u> than yesterday's.
Your article for class treats this problem the <u>most seriously</u>.

1. high   Anderson can jump _____ than Schwartz.

Of all the contestants, Smith jumps the

_____ .

2. badly   I play _____ than she does.

You play the _____ of all.

3. late   They came _____ than I did.

Of all the guests, Barry came the _____ .

4. well   Martha did _____ than you did.

Agnes did the _____ of all.

5. quickly   Charles completed the assignment

_____ than Eric.

Of all the people in the class, he completed the assign-

ment the _____ .

Check your answers on page 30 in the Answer Key for Book Two. If you correctly answered 4 of 5 items, go to Subskill 7E. If not, ask your instructor for help.

Subskill 7E: Choosing Between Adjectives and Adverbs

When you complete this subskill, you will be able to choose the correct adjective or adverb form required in a sentence.

You have learned that predicate adjectives follow linking verbs. You have learned that adverbs modify action verbs. Notice how the words <u>steady</u> and <u>steadily</u> are used below.

The work was steady.

<u>Steady</u> is a predicate adjective following the linking verb <u>was</u>. It modifies the noun <u>work</u>.

We worked steadily.

<u>Steadily</u> is an adverb modifying the action verb <u>worked</u>. It tells how we worked.

You use adjectives after linking verbs and adverbs after action verbs. Some verbs can be either action verbs or linking verbs, depending on how they are used. These include <u>look</u>, <u>feel</u>, <u>taste</u>, and <u>smell</u>. When they are used as linking verbs, they are followed by adjectives. When they are used as action verbs, they are followed by adverbs.

The child looked <u>shy</u>.

<u>Shy</u> is a predicate adjective following the linking verb <u>looked</u>. <u>Shy</u> describes the noun <u>child</u>. The sentence does not tell you what the child did. It describes the child.

The child looked at us <u>shyly</u>.

<u>Shyly</u> is an adverb modifying the action verb <u>looked</u>. This sentence tells you what the child did.

The soup tasted <u>delicious</u>.

<u>Delicious</u> is a predicate adjective following the linking verb <u>tasted</u>. <u>Delicious</u> describes the noun <u>soup</u>. The sentence does not tell you what the soup did. It describes the soup.

I tasted the soup <u>carefully</u>.

<u>Carefully</u> is an adverb modifying the action verb <u>tasted</u>. <u>Carefully</u> tells how I tasted the soup. <u>Tasted</u> is an action verb because it tells what I did.

To test whether <u>looked</u>, <u>tasted</u>, <u>smelled</u>, and <u>felt</u> are being used as linking verbs, substitute the linking verb <u>seem</u> for them. If they are being used as linking verbs, the sentence will still make sense.

You looked (<u>happy</u>, happily).

You seemed (<u>happy</u>, happily).

When you substitute <u>seemed</u> for <u>looked</u>, the sentence still makes sense. <u>Looked</u> is a linking verb in this sentence. Therefore, you should choose the adjective <u>happy</u>, rather than the adverb <u>happily</u>.

I <u>looked</u> over the work   (careful, carefully).

I <u>seemed</u> over the work   (careful, carefully).

When you substitute <u>seemed</u> for <u>looked</u>, the sentence does not make sense. That means that <u>looked</u> is being used as an action verb in the sentence. You should choose the adverb <u>carefully</u> rather than the adjective <u>careful</u>.

Apply what you have learned about choosing adjectives or adverbs by doing the following exercise.

Exercise for Subskill 7E

In each of the sentences below, underline the verb or verb phrase. Then underline the correct word in parentheses. If the verb is a linking verb, underline an adjective. If the verb is an action verb, underline an adverb.

EXAMPLE: She <u>works</u> (diligent, <u>diligently</u>).

1. I crept (cautious, cautiously) across the hall.

2. That looks (terrible, terribly).

3. Bob can jump five feet (easy, easily).

4. This chair feels (comfortable, comfortably).

5. Monica walked (quick, quickly) to work.

6. People today dance (different, differently).

7. The day passed (rapid, rapidly).

8. The television sounds too (loud, loudly).

9. Roses smell (sweet, sweetly).

10. The satin felt (soft, softly).

11. The bus driver has driven (safe, safely) for ten years.

12. I felt the broken leg (cautious, cautiously).

13. I felt (sad, sadly) about losing.

14. The contestants looked (eager, eagerly) at the prizes.

15. The contestants looked (eager, eagerly) to begin.

Check your answers on page 30 in the Answer Key for Book Two. If you correctly answered all 15 items, go to Subskill 7F. If not, do the Supplemental Exercise for Subskill 7E.

Supplemental Exercise for Subskill 7E

Review the information about adjectives and adverbs on pages 153–154. Then do the following exercise.

In each of the sentences below, underline the verb or verb phrase. Then underline the correct word in parentheses. If the verb is a linking verb, underline an adjective. If the verb is an action verb, underline an adverb.

EXAMPLE: The ballerina <u>danced</u> (graceful, <u>gracefully</u>).

1. Please handle the glasses (careful, carefully).

2. The travelers became (weary, wearily).

3. I tasted the pies (eager, eagerly).

4. The pie tastes (terrible, terribly).

5. You look (different, differently) today.

6. Jane looks at things (different, differently).

7. Your response was (prompt, promptly).

8. You responded (prompt, promptly).

9. The homemade bread smelled (wonderful, wonderfully).

10. Artie looked (happy, happily).

Check your answers on page 30 in the Answer Key for Book Two. If you correctly answered 8 of 10 items, go to Subskill 7F. If not, ask your instructor for help.

Subskill 7F: Usage Problems With Certain Adverbs

When you complete this subskill, you will be able to use correctly certain adverbs that are often confused with adjectives. You will also be able to use correctly negative adverbs and the adverbs <u>anywhere</u>, <u>nowhere</u>, <u>somewhere</u>, <u>anyway</u>, <u>rarely</u>, and <u>seldom</u>.

Several adverbs are often misused. Sometimes an adverb is confused with an adjective that is similar. People may get in the habit of using an incorrect form that is very similar to the correct form. The following examples will help you avoid misusing certain adverbs.

(1) Some pairs of adverbs and adjectives are frequently confused. Study the following examples. <u>Really</u> is always an adverb. Use it to modify adjectives and other adverbs.

That poem is <u>really</u> beautiful.

Real is always an adjective. Use it to modify nouns and pronouns.

That is a <u>real</u> pearl.

<u>Well</u> is usually an adverb. It is used as an adjective only when it means the opposite of <u>sick.</u> <u>Good</u> is always an adjective. It should never be used as an adverb.

She plays the piano <u>well</u>. (adverb)

I feel <u>good</u> about my work. (adjective, opposite of bad).

I feel <u>well</u> today. (adjective, opposite of sick)

<u>Badly</u> is an adverb. <u>Bad</u> is an adjective.

I played <u>badly</u> that day.

The fish tasted <u>bad</u>.

(2)   Do not add an <u>s</u> to the adverbs <u>anywhere</u>, <u>nowhere</u>, <u>somewhere</u>, or <u>anyway</u>.

INCORRECT: I can't find my book <u>anywheres</u>.

CORRECT: I can't find my book <u>anywhere</u>.

INCORRECT: She isn't coming <u>anyways</u>.

CORRECT: She isn't coming <u>anyway</u>.

(3)   The word <u>ever</u> does not add anything to the meanings of the words <u>rarely</u> and <u>seldom</u>. Do not use <u>ever</u> with these two adverbs.

INCORRECT: I <u>seldom</u> ever see him.

CORRECT: I <u>seldom</u> see him.

INCORRECT: I <u>rarely</u> ever shop there.

CORRECT: I <u>rarely</u> shop there.

(4)   If you use a negative adverb, do not use another negative word in a negative statement. If you do use another negative word in a statement, do not use a negative adverb.

NOTE: The contraction <u>n't</u> is the negative adverb <u>not</u> attached to the verb. Negative adverbs include <u>not</u> (and the contraction <u>n't</u>), <u>nowhere</u>, <u>hardly</u>, <u>scarcely</u>, and <u>never</u>. Other negative words include <u>no</u>, <u>no one</u>, <u>none</u>, <u>nobody</u>, <u>nothing</u>, and <u>neither</u>.

INCORRECT: I don't have none.

CORRECT: I don't have any.

CORRECT: I have none.

INCORRECT: I can't hardly see.

CORRECT: I can hardly see.

INCORRECT: We never go nowhere.

CORRECT: We never go anywhere.

Exercise for Subskill 7F

Underline the correct word in parentheses.

EXAMPLE: You (<u>have</u>, haven't) hardly touched your dinner.

1. I'm (real, really) tired.

2. It works (good, well).

3. She is hardly (ever, never) depressed.

4. He (could, couldn't) hardly move.

5. I feel (bad, badly) about what happened.

6. Grace lives (somewhere, somewheres) near Boston.

7. Herbie (seldom, seldom ever) calls me.

8. I don't see (anything, nothing) wrong with it.

9. Hardly (anybody, nobody) showed up.

10. He sings (bad, badly).

Check your answers on pages 30 and 31 in the Answer Key for Book Two. If you correctly answered all 10 items, go to the Self-Check. If not, do the Supplemental Exercise for Subskill 7F.

Supplemental Exercise for Subskill 7F

Review the usage examples on pages 155–157. Then do the following exercise.

Each of the following sentences contains at least one error in usage. Rewrite each sentence correctly on the line below.

EXAMPLE: It doesn't matter anyways.

<u>It doesn't matter anyway.</u>

1. Their son sings very bad.

_____

2. You aren't going nowheres.

_____

3. We hardly never have enough money.

_____

4. I did real good on my English exam.

_____

5. It rarely ever snows before Christmas.

_____

Check your answers on page 31 in the Answer Key for Book Two. If you correctly answered 4 of 5 items, go to the Self-Check. If not, ask your instructor for help.

SELF–CHECK: SKILL UNIT 7

Three of the four sentences in each group below are correct. One sentence in each group contains incorrect usage. Circle the letter of the incorrect sentence. Then rewrite the sentence correctly in the space provided.

EXAMPLE: **(a)** Keep your classwork neat.
              (b) Juan finally feels good.
              (c) Eileen runs faster than Tim and Alexandra.
              (d) The baby can hardly stand alone.
              Juan finally feels well.

1. **(a)** Draw the line straight.
    (b) Millie works as fast as she can.
    (c) Of my three brothers, Jimmy drives the most carefully.
    (d) I have not scarcely moved from this desk since lunch.

_____

2. **(a)** We treated you fair.
    (b) Must you speak so sharply?
    (c) We were somewhat tired after our trip.
    (d) Bob was really anxious when he heard the horrible news.

_____

3. (a) My stomach hurt badly last night, but I feel much better today.
   (b) He comes here more oftener than we do.
   (c) This old shoe smells really bad.
   (d) These dogs usually live longer than ten years.

4. (a) We did our work separate.
   (b) I couldn't find it anywhere.
   (c) Thank you for replying promptly.
   (d) He answered me angrily.

5. (a) The store detective looked carefully at the shoplifter.
   (b) I really can't say which of the two I like best.
   (c) Jennifer studies well at school but better at home.
   (d) All four men play tennis well, but Don plays the best.

6. (a) She's fixing her hair different now.
   (b) You look different now.
   (c) Alan plays basketball badly.
   (d) James suffered miserably all day with a toothache, but he's better tonight.

7. (a) There's not nothing wrong with you!
   (b) Sugarless drinks always taste bad to me.
   (c) The detective asked the questions abruptly.
   (d) I could hardly see anything in the dark room.

8. (a) Because of the noise, Mark could scarcely study.
   (b) My cold is more worser today than it was yesterday.
   (c) I've heard several times that you bowl really well.
   (d) Her testimony sounds extremely suspicious to me.

9. (a) Are you real sure you want this car?
   (b) Jennie is the more cooperative of the two children.
   (c) The room seems quiet this time of day.
   (d) The room smelled bad.

10. (a) I seldom see you anymore.
    (b) I wasn't well when you came to see me.
    (c) We won this game easy, but the previous game was much more difficult.
    (d) That joke sounded funnier the first time I heard it.

Check your answers on page 31 in the Answer Key for Book Two. If you correctly answered 8 of 10 items, you have mastered these skills. If not, ask your instructor for help.

Skill Unit 8
USING PREPOSITIONAL PHRASES AS MODIFIERS

What Skills You Need to Begin: You need to be able to identify nouns (Skill Unit 1), verbs (Skill Unit 3), adjectives (Skill Unit 6), and adverbs (Skill Unit 7).

What Skills You Will Learn: After completing this skill unit, you will be able to identify prepositional phrases and use them correctly in sentences.

Why You Need These Skills: Prepositional phrases act as modifiers in a sentence. They can be used as either adjectives or adverbs. Like single-word modifiers, prepositional phrases allow us to describe people, places, things, and actions completely and exactly. They help show how different parts of a sentence relate to each other. You use prepositional phrases every day in speaking and writing. Learning more about their use as modifiers will help you say and write exactly what you mean.

How You Will Show What You Have Learned: You will take the Self-Check at the end of this unit on page 169. The Self-Check consists of 25 items. If you answer 20 of 25 items correctly, you will have shown that you have mastered these skills.

If you feel that you have already mastered these skills, turn to the end of this unit and complete the Self-Check on page 169.

Subskill 8A: Identifying Prepositional Phrases

When you complete this subskill, you will be able to identify prepositional phrases. You will be able to identify the preposition and the object of the preposition that make up each prepositional phrase.

A prepositional phrase is a group of words that begins with a preposition and ends with a noun or pronoun. A preposition is a word that shows relationship. It shows the relationship between the noun or pronoun that follows it in the phrase and some other word in the sentence. **The noun or pronoun that follows the preposition is called the object of the preposition.**

The following sentence contains a prepositional phrase:

Prep Phrase
The pen on the desk is mine.

On the desk is the prepositional phrase. On is the preposition. It shows the relationship between the pen and
the desk. Desk is the object of the preposition.

Now look at these sentences. Notice how changing the preposition
changes the relationship between the pen and the desk.

Prep Phrase
The pen under the desk is mine.

Prep Phrase
The pen behind the desk is mine.

Prep Phrase
The pen near the desk is mine.

Here is another group of sentences containing prepositional
phrases. Notice again how changing the preposition changes the relationship expressed in the sentence.

Prep Phrase
I took the present from Becky.

Prep Phrase
I took the present to Becky.

Prep Phrase
I took the present for Becky.

Study the following list of words that can be used as prepositions.

aboard	at	down	of	under
about	before	during	off	underneath
above	behind	except	on	until
across	below	for	over	up
after	beneath	from	past	upon
against	beside	in	since	with
along	between	into	through	within
amid	beyond	like	throughout	without
among	but	near	to	
around	by		toward	

Some prepositions are made up of more than one word. Study the
following list.

according to	because of	instead of
along with	by way of	on account of
apart from	except for	on top of
as far as	in regard to	out of
aside from	in addition to	together with
as to	in spite of	

Many of the words on the list of prepositions can also be used as adverbs. When the words are followed by a noun or pronoun used as an object, they are prepositions. When they are not followed by an object, they are adverbs.

NOTE: Throughout this unit, an object of a preposition will be labeled O Prep.

Prep   O Prep
The boy fell down the stairs.

Down the stairs is a prepositional phrase. Down is the preposition and stairs is the object of the preposition.

Adv
The boy fell down.

There is no prepositional phrase. Down is an adverb in this sentence. To be used as a preposition, down must be followed by a noun or pronoun that is the object of the preposition.

Exercise for Subskill 8A

For each sentence, do the following:

- Underline the prepositional phrase or phrases.
- Circle the preposition in each phrase.
- Write O Prep over the object of each preposition.

Review your work to be sure you have completed each step. Some sentences contain more than one prepositional phrase.

O Prep   O Prep
EXAMPLE: A man (with) gray hair was standing (beside) Lois.

1. The water in the bay was very cold.

2. She ran across the busy street.

3. I went to the party with some friends.

4. I voted for Laura because of your advice.

5. You can do this exercise without any help.

6. They have lived in St. Louis since last year.

7. He fell off his bike.

8. I found some crackers in the bottom of the box.

9. We went outside and looked at the stars.

10. Everyone is coming over, except for Jennifer.

Check your answers on page 31 in the Answer Key for Book Two. If you correctly answered all 10 items, go to Subskill 8B. If not, do the Supplemental Exercise for Subskill 8A.

Supplemental Exercise for Subskill 8A

Review the information about prepositional phrases on pages 161–163. Then do the following exercise.

For each sentence, do the following:

· Underline the prepositional phrase or phrases.

· Circle the preposition in each phrase.

· Write O Prep over the object of each preposition.

Review your work to be sure you have completed each step. Some sentences contain more than one prepositional phrase.

EXAMPLE: I voted (against) the first issue (on) the ballot.

1. I talked to Alan during my break.

2. Rachel keeps dishes on the top shelf of the cupboard.

3. The street below my window is always noisy.

4. We went to a movie on Sunday.

5. The person beside John was sitting down.

6. He took a train from Baltimore to New York.

7. John went for a walk with his wife after dinner.

8. They were continuing the game in spite of the bad weather.

9.   Helen told me about your accident.

10.   The top spun around and landed against the wall.

Check your answers on page 31 in the Answer Key for Book Two. If you correctly answered 8 of 10 items, go to Subskill 8B. If not, ask your instructor for help.

Subskill 8B: Using Prepositional Phrases Effectively

When you complete this subskill, you will be able to identify prepositional phrases that function as adjectives and prepositional phrases that function as adverbs. You will be able to position prepositional phrases carefully so that it is clear which word in a sentence a prepositional phrase modifies.

Prepositional Phrases Are Modifiers

Some prepositional phrases function as adjectives. They help describe a noun or pronoun. Prepositional phrases functioning as adjectives usually answer the question "Which one?" (See Skill Unit 6 to review the questions that adjectives answer.)

Prep Phrase
The items on the top shelf are dusty.

Which items? The items on the top shelf. On the top shelf is a prepositional phrase functioning as an adjective. The phrase modifies the noun items. It tells which ones.

Other prepositional phrases function as adverbs. They modify the verb by answering the questions "Where?" "When?" or "How?" (See Skill Unit 7 to review the questions adverbs answer.)

Prep Phrase
I put the book on the top shelf.

Put the book where? On the top shelf. On the top shelf is a prepositional phrase functioning as an adverb. The phrase modifies the verb put.

Prep Phrase
I will meet you after work.

Will meet when? After work. After work is a prepositional phrase functioning as an adverb. It modifies the verb meet.

Prep Phrase
He cut the string with a knife.

Cut how? With a knife. <u>With a knife</u> is a prepositional phrase functioning as an adverb. It modifies the verb <u>cut</u>.

Using Prepositional Phrases to Say What You Mean

The position of a prepositional phrase in a sentence is important. Notice how changing the position of the prepositional phrase changes the meaning of the following sentences.

Prep Prase
The man with the dark hair said hello to the woman.

Which man? The man <u>with the dark hair</u>. The prepositional phrase functions as an adjective that modifies the noun <u>man</u>.

Prep Phrase
The man said hello to the woman with the dark hair.

Which woman? The woman <u>with the dark hair</u>. The prepositional phrase functions as an adjective that modifies the noun <u>woman</u>.

Prep Phrase
Those people across the street are moving.

Which people? The people <u>across the street</u>. The prepositional phrase functions as an adjective that modifies the noun <u>people</u>.

Prep Phrase
Those people are moving across the street.

Moving where? <u>Across the street</u>. The prepositional phrase functions as an adverb that modifies the verb <u>moving</u>.

Sometimes prepositional phrases functioning as adverbs may be moved around in a sentence without affecting the meaning of the sentence.

Prep Phrase
During the summer, we go swimming often.

Prep Phrase
We go swimming often during the summer.

Often, however, you must be careful where you position the phrase or you may confuse your readers.

DON'T SAY: <u>On top of the cake</u>, we were sprinkling coconut.

Since the word <u>we</u> follows the prepositional phrase, this sentence seems to say that we were on top of the cake.

SAY: We were sprinkling coconut <u>on top of the cake</u>.

DON'T SAY: Because of their huge size and ancient history, many tourists are fascinated by the Egyptian pyramids.

This sentence seems to be talking about huge, ancient tourists.

SAY: Many tourists are fascinated by the Egyptian pyramids because of their huge size and ancient history.

Apply what you have learned about positioning prepositional phrases by doing the following exercise.

Exercise for Subskill 8B

Part A.   For each sentence, do the following:

- Underline the prepositional phrase.

- Draw an arrow to the word each phrase modifies.

- In the blank, write adjective if the phrase modifies a noun or pronoun. Write adverb if the phrase modifies a verb.

Review your work to be sure you have completed each step.

EXAMPLE: We drove past the new school.   ____adverb____

1. The picture on the right is beautiful. _____

2. Two strangers were walking toward the house. _____

3. It rained during the night. _____

4. The store around the corner has low prices. _____

5. Jim ran around the block. _____

Part B.   Each of the following sentences contains a prepositional phrase. Read each sentence carefully. If the meaning of the sentence is clear, write C on the line below the sentence. If the meaning of the sentence is not clear, rewrite the sentence on the line, changing the position of the prepositional phrase.

EXAMPLE: We could see many faraway animals with binoculars.

With binoculars, we could see many faraway animals.

6. Steve and Rhonda saw two raccoons on their way home from work.

_____

7. With regret, I said goodbye and drove away.

_____

8. Inside a little wooden box, she hid her valuables.

    _____

9. Because of their soft, cuddly fur, many people find baby animals
    irresistible.

    _____

    _____

10. During the second half, the game got more exciting.

    _____

Check your answers on page 32 in the Answer Key for Book Two.
If you correctly answered all 10 items go to the Self-Check. If not, do
the Supplemental Exercise for Subskill 8B.

Supplemental Exercise for Subskill 8B

Review the information about using prepositional phrases on pages
165–167. Then do the following exercise.

Part A. For each sentence, do the following:

- Underline the prepositional phrase.

- Draw an arrow to the word each phrase modifies.

- In the blank, write <u>adjective</u> if the phrase modifies a noun or
  pronoun. Write <u>adverb</u> if the phrase modifies a verb.

Review your work to be sure you have completed each step.

EXAMPLE: The latch <u>on the suitcase</u> was broken.   ___adjective___

1. She walked home from the bus station.   _____

2. Two people from my department have been promoted.

    _____

3. I will call after dinner.   _____

4. I forget the name of that song.   _____

5. Throughout the night, the nurse checked on the patient.

    _____

Part B. Each of the sentences on page 169 contains a prepositional
phrase. Read each sentence carefully. If the meaning of the sentence is
clear, write <u>C</u> on the line below the sentence. If the meaning of the
sentence is not clear, rewrite the sentence on the line, changing the
position of the prepositional phrase.

EXAMPLE: Above our heads, some hawks were flying.

_____C_____

6. In spite of their leaky pipes and crumbling plaster, many people like old houses.

_____

7. Inside the cage, we looked at the hungry lion.
(The lion was in the cage, but we weren't!)

_____

8. After the game, we went dancing.

_____

9. On top of the mountain, we had our lunch.

_____

10. With a loud thud, I heard the heavy box fall.

_____

Check your answers on pages 32 and 33 in the Answer Key for Book Two. If you correctly answered 8 of 10 items correctly, go to the Self-Check. If not, ask your instructor for help.

SELF–CHECK: SKILL UNIT 8

Part A.   For each sentence, do the following:

- Underline all of the prepositional phrases.

- Circle the prepositions.

- Write O Prep above each object of the preposition.

Review your work to be sure you have completed each step.

EXAMPLE: The end (of) the rope was dangling (over) the edge (of) the desk.

1. I slid across the ice and fell down.

2. Anna came with me to the store, but she stayed in the car.

3. After the last race, the runner collapsed on the track.

4. The aisle between the seats was too narrow.

5. The label on the back of the box listed all of the ingredients in the product.

6. We drove from our house to Detroit in three hours.

7. During the last inning, our team fell behind.

8. Before lunch, the children played outside.

9. The pencil fell off the table and rolled behind a cabinet.

10. That movie about dolphins will be playing at the theatre until tomorrow.

Part B. For each sentence, do the following:
  - Underline the prepositional phrase.
  - Draw an arrow to the word each phrase modifies.
  - In the blank, write <u>adjective</u> if the phrase modifies a noun or pronoun. Write <u>adverb</u> if the phrase modifies a verb.

Review your work to be sure you have completed each step.

EXAMPLE: The boy in the middle is my son. _____adjective_____

11. After the argument, she apologized. _____

12. The ball crashed through the window. _____

13. My cousin from New York is visiting me. _____

14. Our neighbors down the hall are coming. _____

15. Our neighbors are coming down the hall. _____

16. The instructions to the game are lost. _____

17. The debate between the two candidates was interesting.

_____

18. He jumped into the pool and swam two laps. _____

19. Margie works at the factory. _____

20. I like the jacket with the hood. _____

Part C.   Each of the following sentences contains a prepositional phrase. Read each sentence carefully. If the meaning of the sentence is clear, write C on the line below the sentence. If the meaning of the sentence is not clear, rewrite the sentence on the line, changing the position of the prepositional phrase.

EXAMPLE: The girls went outside to see the snowflakes with their heavy coats on.

<u>   With their heavy coats on, the girls went outside to see   </u>
<u>   the snowflakes.   </u>

21.   Inside the tiny hole, I saw a mouse.

_____

22.   With a sigh of relief, I finished the job and went home.

_____

23.   Because of the bad weather, we cancelled our picnic.

_____

24.   Al and Shirley saw a flock of geese on their way to work.

_____

25.   With blaring sirens, we heard the fire trucks arrive.

_____

Check your answers on pages 33 and 34 in the Answer Key for Book Two. If you correctly answered 20 of 25 items, you have mastered these skills. If not, ask your instructor for help.

Skill Unit 9
IDENTIFYING SIMPLE SENTENCE PATTERNS

What Skills You Need to Begin: You need to be able to identify nouns (Skill Unit 1), verbs (Skill Unit 3), adjectives (Skill Unit 6), adverbs (Skill Unit 7), and prepositional phrases (Skill Unit 8).

What Skills You Will Learn: After completing this skill unit, you will be able to identify the three basic sentence patterns that can be formed with action verbs and the two basic sentence patterns that can be formed with linking verbs. You will also be able to identify the sentence parts of "troublesome" sentences.

Why You Need These Skills: You have learned that the basic unit for communicating a complete thought is called the simple sentence. Every language has rules about how to put words together to communicate meaning. Children learn the sentence patterns of a language by imitating other speakers. They aren't aware of the rules and patterns they are following. Now that you have learned about nouns, verbs, adjectives, adverbs, and prepositional phrases, however, you can take another look at the kinds of sentences you use every day. You can understand the rules and patterns you follow to combine these elements into meaningful sentences. In this unit you will learn that there are five basic ways for simple sentences to be put together in English. Once you learn to recognize these patterns, you will be ready to recognize more complex sentence structures. Each sentence pattern offers different possibilities for expressing yourself in English. As you become more familiar with all the possibilities offered by different sentence patterns, you will be able to communicate in more effective and interesting ways.

How You Will Show What You Have Learned: You will take the Self-Check at the end of this unit on page 188. The Self-Check consists of 20 items. If you answer 16 of 20 items correctly, you will have shown that you have mastered these skills.

If you feel that you have already mastered these skills, turn to the end of this unit and complete the Self-Check on page 188.

Subskill 9A: Identifying Action Verb Sentence Patterns

When you complete this subskill, you will be able to identify the three basic action verb sentence patterns. You will also be able to identify sentences that contain these patterns even when the sentences contain modifiers and compound parts.

The Subject + Action Verb Pattern

One **simple sentence** pattern consists of a subject and an action verb. In the examples, S = subject and AV = action verb.

$$\text{S} \quad \text{AV}$$
The boys jumped.

$$\text{S} \quad \quad \text{AV}$$
The woman is laughing.

This simple sentence pattern may be expanded by adding modifiers to either or both parts.

$$\text{S} \quad \quad \quad \text{AV}$$
The little boys in the park jumped up in excitement.

$$\text{S} \quad \quad \quad \text{AV}$$
The old woman behind me is laughing hysterically.

Notice that the basic pattern of each sentence is still the same.

The S + AV pattern may also be expanded by adding an additional subject and/or verb. **When two or more subjects share the same verb, the sentence has a compound subject.**

$$\text{S} \quad \quad \text{S} \quad \quad \text{AV}$$
The little boys and girls in the park jumped up in excitement.

$$\text{S} \quad \quad \quad \text{S} \quad \text{AV}$$
The old woman and her friend are laughing hysterically.

When one subject is joined to two or more verbs, the sentence has a **compound verb.**

$$\text{S} \quad \quad \quad \text{AV} \quad \quad \text{AV}$$
The little boys in the park jumped up and ran away.

$$\text{S} \quad \quad \quad \text{AV} \quad \quad \text{AV}$$
The old woman behind me is laughing and talking.

When two or more subjects share two or more verbs, the sentence has a compound subject and a compound verb.

S   S   AV   AV
The little boys and girls in the park jumped up and ran away.

S   S   AV   AV
The old woman and her friend are laughing and talking.

Every sentence you have studied so far follows the same basic sentence pattern: Subject + Action Verb (S + AV). Any additional words in the sentence are modifiers. Notice how each sentence fits into the following chart.

S	AV
boys	jumped
woman	is laughing
boys and girls	jumped
woman and friend	are laughing
boys	jumped and ran
woman	is laughing and talking
boys and girls	jumped and ran
woman and friend	are laughing and talking

Apply what you have learned by doing the following exercise.

Exercise 1 for Subskill 9A

Each of the following sentences uses the basic S + AV pattern. Find the subject and the verb of each sentence. Write them in the chart below. If the sentence contains a compound subject or compound verb, write both subjects or verbs and include the words <u>and</u> or <u>or</u> as part of the subject or verb. Do not write any modifiers in the chart.

	S	AV
EXAMPLE:	Mary and brother	were walking
1.		
2.		
3.		
4.		
5.		

EXAMPLE: Mary and my brother were walking in the park.

1.   That shy man at the next table eats too fast.
2.   I dressed quickly and went out.
3.   The people on the elevator stared straight ahead.
4.   Jesse and Amy are talking quietly and smiling at each other.
5.   Either the new supervisor or her assistant will come in early.

Check your answers on page 34 in the Answer Key for Book Two. If you correctly answered all 5 items, continue reading. If not, review the discussion about basic S + AV sentence patterns on pages 173–174. Then go on to the next section of Subskill 9A. NOTE: The skills in this exercise will be used in some of the sentences in the Supplemental Exercise for Subskill 9A on page 179.

The Subject + Action Verb + Direct Object Pattern

Some sentences need more than a subject, a verb, and modifiers to express a complete thought. Look at these examples:

Howard is taking _____ .

The tall player in the blue uniform hit _____ .

Rachel thanked _____ .

In each of the examples, something is missing. We want to know what Howard took, what the player hit, and whom Rachel thanked. Each of the sentences needs a **direct object.**

A direct object is a noun or pronoun that tells who or what receives the action of the verb. You will learn about pronouns as direct objects in the next unit. In this unit, you will study nouns as direct objects.

Now look at the examples with direct objects filled in. In the examples, S = subject, AV = action verb, and DO = direct object.

     S   AV   DO
Howard is taking his turn.

         S   AV   DO
The tall player in the blue uniform hit the ball to center field.

   S   AV   DO
Rachel thanked her friends for all their help.

Each of the three sentences has the same basic pattern.

S	AV	DO
Howard	is taking	turn
player	hit	ball
Rachel	thanked	friends

Sentences with the S + AV + DO pattern can have compound subjects, compound verbs, or compound direct objects.

      S   S   AV   DO
Howard and Mark are taking their turns.

       S   AV   DO
The player in the blue uniform hit the ball to center field and
AV   DO
threw the bat to the ground.

     S   AV   DO   DO
Rachel thanked her family and friends.

Here is how the sentences would look in the chart.

S	AV	DO
Howard and Mark	are taking	turns
player	hit (and)	ball
	threw	bat
Rachel	thanked	family and friends

Look carefully at the second sentence. Each of the verbs has its own direct object. Compare that sentence to the third sentence. Here, the compound direct object shares the same verb.

The Subject + Action Verb + Indirect Object + Direct Object Pattern

Look at these sentences.

   S   AV   DO
She gave ———————— three dollars.

   S   AV   DO
Bill told ———————— a very funny joke.

        S   AV   DO
The husband bought ———————— a present.

Each sentence already has a subject, an action verb, and a direct object. Still, something could be added to each sentence. We could tell to whom she gave three dollars, to whom Bill told a joke, and for whom the husband bought a present.

To add this information to each sentence, we can fill in an indirect object. An **indirect object** usually tells to whom or for whom an action is done. Sometimes it tells to what or for what an action is done.

Now look at the sentences with indirect objects filled in. In the examples, S = subject, AV = action verb, IO = indirect object, and DO = direct object.

    S   AV   IO   DO
She gave her sister three dollars.

    S   AV IO   IO   DO
Bill told Marv and Angie a very funny joke.

         S   AV   IO   DO
The husband bought his wife a present.

Here is how the sentences would look in a sentence pattern chart.

S	AV	IO	DO
She	gave	sister	dollars
Bill	told	Marv and Angie	joke
husband	bought	wife	present

As you can see from the chart, a sentence may have a compound indirect object.

Finding Direct Objects and Indirect Objects

An indirect object can appear only in combination with a direct object. It never appears alone. To find out if a sentence has an indirect object, first determine whether it has a direct object—a word that tells who or what receives the action. If you find a direct object, then ask whether there is also a word that tells to whom or for whom the action is done. Look at the following example:

We sent Isabel a long letter.

(1)   You know that the subject is <u>we</u> and the action verb is <u>sent</u>.

(2)   Now find the direct object by asking whom or what did we send? Did we send Isabel? No. We sent the letter. <u>Letter</u> is the direct object.

(3)   You know that the sentence has a direct object. That means it may also have an indirect object. Find out whether it does by asking if the sentence tells to whom or for whom we sent the letter. To whom did we send the letter? We sent the letter to Isabel. <u>Isabel</u> is the indirect object.

S	AV	IO	DO
We	sent	Isabel	letter

Notice that the indirect object always comes between the action verb and the direct object.

NOTE: The words to and for are never expressed before an indirect object. If the words to and for are expressed before the object, then the sentence has a prepositional phrase rather than an indirect object.

S   AV   DO
We sent a long letter to Isabel.

In this sentence, the pattern is S + AV + DO. To Isabel is a prepositional phrase modifying the verb sent. Isabel is the object of the preposition to.

Exercise 2 for Subskill 9A

Each of the following sentences fits one of the patterns you have learned so far:

S + AV

S + AV + DO

S + AV + IO + DO

Fill in the chart below with the subject and action verb of each sentence. If the sentence includes a word that tells who or what received the action—a direct object—write that word in the DO column. If the sentence also contains an indirect object, write that word in the IO column. Ignore all modifiers and prepositional phrases. Some sentences contain compound parts. If a part is a compound, include the word and in the chart.

	S	AV	IO	DO
EXAMPLES:	Herb and Alice mechanic	are painting worked		kitchen
1.				
2.				
3.				
4.				
5.				
6.				
7.				
8.				
9.				
10.				

EXAMPLES: Herb and Alice are painting the kitchen.
The young mechanic worked hard all day.

1. The women at the office gave Roberta a party.
2. The three brothers were sitting outside under a shady tree.
3. Her hungry children ate their soup and drank their milk.
4. Jackson threw the ball to the third baseman.
5. The man with the cane slipped and fell on the icy sidewalk.
6. Marjorie passed her husband the salt.
7. Ron took his vacation in July.
8. The defendant told the truth to the judge.
9. I like peaches and strawberries.
10. We brought the sick man some flowers.

Check your answers on page 34 in the Answer Key for Book Two. If you correctly answered all 10 items, go to Subskill 9B. If not, do the Supplemental Exercise for Subskill 9A.

Supplemental Exercise for Subskill 9A

Review the information about the three basic action verb sentence patterns on pages 173–178. Then do the following exercise.

Fill in the chart below with the subject and action verb in each sentence. If the sentence includes a word that tells who or what received the action—a direct object—write that word in the DO column. If the sentence also contains an indirect object, write that word in the IO column. Ignore all modifiers and prepositional phrases. Some sentences contain compound parts. If a part is compound, include the word <u>and</u> in the chart.

	S	AV	IO	DO
EXAMPLES:	We	gave	dog	bath
1.				
2.				
3.				
4.				
5.				
6.				
7.				
8.				
9.				
10.				

EXAMPLE: We gave our frisky dog a bath.

1. The quarterback caught the pass and made a touchdown.
2. Harold threw Joe the keys.
3. She has wanted a new car for a long time.
4. Our friend from Pittsburgh is going to school and studying hard.
5. Our friend from Pittsburgh is studying electronics.
6. I made my daughter a sweater.
7. Sheila and Bob took their friend to the airport.
8. We really enjoyed the dessert and the coffee.
9. The next express train will be arriving in about five minutes.
10. Carol is lending her neighbors a stepladder.

Check your answers on pages 34 and 35 in the Answer Key for Book Two. If you correctly answered 8 of 10 items, go to Subskill 9B. If not, ask your instructor for help.

Subskill 9B: Identifying Linking Verb Sentence Patterns

When you complete this subskill, you will be able to identify linking verb sentence patterns.

Linking Verb Sentence Patterns

You learned in Skill Unit 3 that linking verbs do not show action (Subskill 3D). Instead, they link the subject to a word that renames or describes the subject.

A noun that follows a linking verb and renames the subject is called a predicate noun. The following sentence has the pattern subject + linking verb + predicate noun (S + LV + PN).

S   LV   PN
Shirley was the winner of the race.

Sometimes the word that renames the subject is a predicate pronoun. You will learn more about predicate pronouns in the next unit.

An adjective that follows a linking verb and describes the subject is called a predicate adjective. The following sentence has the pattern subject + linking verb + predicate adjective (S + LV + PA).

S   LV   PA
Shirley was tired after the race.

Identifying Linking Verbs

(1) Remember that all the forms of the verb <u>be</u> (<u>am</u>, <u>is</u>, <u>are</u>, <u>was</u>, <u>were</u>, <u>be</u>, <u>being</u>, <u>been</u>) can be linking verbs. They can also be helping verbs in a verb phrase.

      S LV   PN
      Jan was the leader of the trip.

      S LV PA
      Jan was sorry.

      S   AV
      Jan was going to work.

      S   LV   PA
      Jan was being stubborn.

If you need more help in distinguishing linking verbs from helping verbs, review Subskill 3E.

(2) Remember that the verbs <u>seem</u> and <u>become</u> are always linking verbs. The verb <u>appear</u> can be a linking verb or an action verb.

      S LV PA
      You seem restless.

      S   LV   PN
      Ramon became a medical technician.

      S   AV
      Suddenly, a rabbit appeared inside the magician's hat.

      S   LV   PA
      Randy appeared embarrassed.

(3) Remember that the verbs <u>feel</u>, <u>taste</u>, <u>smell</u>, <u>look</u>, <u>sound</u>, and <u>grow</u> may be either linking verbs or action verbs.

      S LV PA
      I felt happy.

      S AV   DO
      I felt the wet paint.

If you need more help in distinguishing linking verbs from action verbs, review Subskill 3F.

Apply what you have learned by doing the following exercise. You will need to apply what you learned about action verb patterns in Subskill 9A as well as what you have just learned about linking verb patterns.

Exercise for Subskill 9B

Each of the following sentences contains either a linking verb pattern or an action verb pattern. Fill in the correct parts of the chart for each sentence.

	S	LV	AV	PA	PN	IO	DO
EXAMPLES:	They	will be		angry			
	They		will be planning				picnic
1.							
2.							
3.							
4.							
5.							
6.							
7.							
8.							
9.							
10.							

EXAMPLES: They will be angry about the score.
They will be planning a picnic for next Sunday.

1. Anna is tasting the stew.
2. The stew tastes too spicy.
3. Terry was telling his friends a funny story.
4. You are a good driver.
5. Becky is usually grumpy in the mornings.
6. Your friend is looking tired.
7. Your friend is looking at the pictures.
8. The red shirt was my first choice.

9. The man in the back row seems confused.
10. We grew bored with the discussion after a while.

Check your answers on page 35 in the Answer Key for Book Two. If you correctly answered all 10 items, go to Subskill 9C. If not, do the Supplemental Exercise for Subskill 9B.

Supplemental Exercise for Subskill 9B

Review the information about linking verb sentence patterns on pages 180–181. You'll also need to remember what you learned about action verb patterns. Then do the following exercise.

Each of the following sentences contains either a linking verb pattern or an action verb pattern. Fill in the correct parts of the chart for each sentence.

	S	LV	AV	PA	PN	IO	DO
EXAMPLES:	Andy	is becoming			apprentice		
1.							
2.							
3.							
4.							
5.							
6.							
7.							
8.							
9.							
10.							

EXAMPLE: Andy is becoming a carpenter's apprentice.

1. Arthur is growing a beard.
2. We should be grateful for their help.
3. I feel optimistic about our chances.
4. The nurse felt my pulse and took my blood pressure.
5. It has been a long day.
6. Tom has been driving a cab for two years.
7. Your idea sounds interesting.
8. We will be leaving in the morning.
9. She is the worker with the most seniority.
10. June and I smelled leaking gas in the kitchen.

Check your answers on pages 35 and 36 in the Answer Key for Book Two. If you correctly answered 8 of 10 items, go to Subskill 9C. If not, ask your instructor for help.

Subskill 9C: Identifying the Sentence Parts of Special Sentences

When you complete this subskill, you will be able to identify the sentence parts of questions, sentences beginning with <u>here</u> or <u>there</u>, sentences that begin with an adverb or prepositional phrase, and commands.

Questions

In a question, part or all of the verb comes before the subject:

LV   S
Is your answer correct?

AV   S   AV
Did you answer the question correctly?

To find the simple sentence pattern for a question, rewrite the sentence as a statement:

S   LV   PA
Your answer is correct.

S   AV   DO
You did answer the question correctly.

Sentences That Begin With "Here" or "There"

<u>Here</u> and <u>there</u> are never the subjects of a sentence. When sentences begin with <u>here is</u>, <u>there is</u>, <u>here are</u>, or <u>there are</u>, the subject

comes after the verb. To find the subject, rewrite the sentence so that the words <u>is here</u>, <u>is there</u>, <u>are here</u>, or <u>are there</u> come at the end or near the end of the sentence.

                                   S   V

Here is your coffee = Your coffee is here.

There are three good movies in town. = Three good

    S   V

movies are there in town.

Sentences That Begin With an Adverb or Prepositional Phrase

Some sentences begin with an adverb or a prepositional phrase. You know that an adverb or prepositional phrase cannot be the subject of a sentence. In many of these sentences, the subject may come after the verb. You may need to rewrite the sentence to find the subject.

                             S   V

Along came James. = James came along.

In the forest near our camp lives a grizzly bear. =

            S   V

A grizzly bear lives in the forest near our camp.

Commands and Requests

In a command or request, the subject is usually not stated.

Please bake me a cake.

Halt!

Go to the store and buy some milk.

In each of these sentences, we say that the subject <u>you</u> is "understood."

     S   AV IO DO

(You) Please bake me a cake.

     S   AV

(You) Halt!

     S   AV   AV   DO

(You) Go to the store and buy some milk.

Apply what you have learned about troublesome sentences by doing the following exercise.

Exercise for Subskill 9C

Read each sentence carefully and do the following:

- If the sentence parts are not in the usual order, rewrite the sentence on the lines below.
- If the sentence has a subject that is understood, rewrite the sentence, putting the understood subject in parentheses.
- Write S above each subject and V above each verb.

Review your work to be sure you have completed each step.

EXAMPLE: Next to the couch was a lamp.
                                        S   V
             A lamp was next to the couch.

1. Here is your sweater.

    _____

2. Did they bring Mary a sandwich?

    _____

3. Along the side of the road was a hubcap.

    _____

4. Is Jerry the best person for the job?

    _____

5. Stop!

    _____

6. There is a good show on television tonight.

    _____

7. In the middle of the yard stood a stray dog.

    _____

8. Bring me a quart of ice cream.

    _____

9. Are you going to the post office?

    _____

10. Please write down this number.

    _____

Check your answers on page 36 in the Answer Key for Book Two. If you correctly answered all 10 items, go to the Self-Check. If not, do the Supplemental Exercise for Subskill 9C.

Supplemental Exercise for Subskill 9C

Review the information about troublesome sentences on page 185 and page 186. Then do the following exercise.

Read each sentence carefully and do the following:

- If the sentence parts are not in the usual order, rewrite the sentence on the lines below.

- If the sentence has a subject that is understood, rewrite the sentence, putting the understood subject in parentheses.

- Write S above each subject and V above each verb.

Review your work to be sure you have completed each step.

EXAMPLE: Have a seat.

$$\underline{\quad\quad\quad\overset{S}{\quad}\quad\overset{V}{\quad}\quad\quad\quad}$$
(You)   Have a seat.

1. At the bottom of the hill was a small pond.

2. Tell me another joke.

3. Here are your shoes.

4. Did she seem excited about the idea?

5. By the end of the day we were exhausted.

6. Where did he go?

7. Down came a spider.

8. There is a hole in my sock.

_____

9. Are they sending you a package?

_____

10. Please give him another chance.

_____

Check your answers on page 36 in the Answer Key for Book Two. If you correctly answered 8 of 10 items, go to the Self-Check. If not, ask your instructor for help.

SELF–CHECK: SKILL UNIT 9

Part A.   Write the letter of the correct definition in the blank next to each term.

_____ 1. subject

_____ 2. verb

_____ 3. direct object

_____ 4. indirect object

_____ 5. predicate noun or predicate pronoun

_____ 6. predicate adjective

(a) receives the action of the verb

(b) follows a linking verb and describes the subject

(c) tells who or what the sentence is about

(d) follows a linking verb and renames the subject

(e) expresses action or links the subject to a word that renames or describes the subject

(f) tells to whom or for whom an action is done

Part B.   Read each sentence and fill in the sentence parts in the chart below.

EXAMPLES: He made Gail a sandwich.
             They will be planning next year's picnic.

	S	LV	AV	PA	PN	IO	DO
EXAMPLES:	He		made			Gail	sandwich
	They		will be planning				picnic
7.							
8.							

	S	LV	AV	PA	PN	IO	DO
9.							
10.							
11.							
12.							
13.							
14.							
15.							
16.							

7. The boy with the dark hair is my nephew.
8. Call your sister quickly.
9. The boss gave me a raise.
10. The old horse trotted slowly past the barn.
11. I cashed a check and paid my bills.
12. Are you a plumber?
13. Dave, Lisa, and Sam planned a surprise party for their friend.
14. The weather was hot and humid.
15. Have you told Susan the truth?
16. Did he answer your letter?

Part C. Read each sentence and do the following:

- Rewrite the sentence so that the sentence parts are in the usual order.

- Write <u>S</u> above each subject and <u>V</u> above each verb.

Review your work to be sure you have completed each step.

EXAMPLE: Under the bed were three pairs of shoes.

$$\text{\underline{}}$$

                  S   V
Three pairs of shoes were under the bed.

17. Here is your money.

_____

18. In the corner of the room stood a large plant.

_____

19. There are two eggs in the refrigerator.

_____

20. Along came Joe.

_____

Check your answers on pages 36 and 37 in the Answer Key for Book Two. If you correctly answered 16 of 20 items, you have mastered these skills. If not, ask your instructor for help.

Skill Unit 10
USING PRONOUNS CORRECTLY

What Skills You Need to Begin: You need to be able to identify nouns (Skill Unit 1), verbs (Skill Unit 3), prepositional phrases (Skill Unit 8), and simple sentence patterns (Skill Unit 9).

What Skills You Will Learn: Different types of pronouns serve different purposes. After completing this skill unit, you will be able to use various types of pronouns. You will also be able to identify the antecedent of a pronoun and make sure that the pronoun agrees with its antecedent in person, number, and gender.

Why You Need These Skills: Many common usage errors are due to choosing the wrong pronoun. Learning to use pronouns correctly will improve your ability to communicate. It will also improve your performance on tests of Standard English usage. Correct pronoun usage is especially important in job-related situations and if you go on to further study.

How You Will Show What You Have Learned: You will take the Self-Check at the end of this unit on page 221. The Self-Check consists of 20 items. If you correctly answer 16 of 20 items, you will have shown that you have mastered these skills.

If you feel that you have already mastered these skills, turn to the end of this unit and complete the Self-Check on page 221.

Subskill 10A: Using Subject and Object Pronouns Correctly

When you complete this subskill, you will be able to use the pronouns I, you, he, she, it, we, they, me, him, her, us, and them correctly.

191

Personal Pronouns

A pronoun is a word that is used in place of a noun. Pronouns that are used in place of specific persons are called **personal pronouns.** Look at the following sentences:

Jerry wants to see Abby tonight.

He wants to take her to a movie.

The first sentence mentions two nouns: <u>Jerry</u> and <u>Abby</u>. The second sentence contains two pronouns: <u>he</u> and <u>her</u>. The pronoun <u>he</u> is used in place of the noun <u>Jerry</u>. The pronoun <u>her</u> is used in place of the noun <u>Abby</u>.

NOTE: The word that a pronoun is used in place of or refers to is called its **antecedent.** In the sentences above, <u>Jerry</u> is the antecedent of the pronoun <u>he</u>. <u>Abby</u> is the antecedent of the pronoun <u>her</u>. You will learn more about antecedents in Subskills 10D and 10E.

Because personal pronouns are used in place of nouns, they can do the same jobs that nouns do in a sentence. They can be subjects, predicate pronouns, direct objects, indirect objects, and objects of the preposition.

Personal pronouns that can be used as subjects and predicate pronouns are called subject pronouns. Personal pronouns that can be used as direct objects, indirect objects, and objects of the preposition are called object pronouns.

Subject Pronouns

Study the following chart of subject pronouns:

	Singular	Plural
1st Person	I	we
2nd Person	you	you
3rd Person	he, she, it	they

Subject Pronouns May Be Singular or Plural

You have learned that nouns may be singular or plural. So may the pronouns that are used in place of nouns. Notice that the pronouns <u>I</u>, <u>he</u>, <u>she</u>, and <u>it</u> are singular in number. They refer to one person or thing. Notice that the pronouns <u>we</u> and <u>they</u> are plural in number. They refer to more than one person or thing. Notice that the pronoun <u>you</u> may be either singular or plural, depending on whether it refers to one person or more than one.

Subject Pronouns May Be First Person, Second Person, or Third Person

Notice the words first person, second person, and third person down the side of the chart.

The **first person** subject pronouns are I and we. They refer to the person(s) speaking. The **second person** subject pronoun is you. It refers to the person(s) being spoken to. The **third person** subject pronouns are he, she, it, and they. They refer to the person(s) or thing(s) being spoken about.

Some Subject Pronouns Indicate Gender

You know that the third person singular pronouns he and she indicate the sex or gender of the person being spoken about. He is masculine in gender. She is feminine in gender. The pronoun it is used for animals or things that are neither masculine nor feminine. The third person plural pronoun they is used to refer to plural nouns that are masculine, feminine, or both.

Using Subject Pronouns Correctly

Rule 1: Use subject pronouns as the subject of a sentence.

        S   V
        He likes that program.

        S   S   V
        Bob and I went out last night.

        S   V
        She ordered spaghetti.

        S   V
        We are waiting for a bus.

Rule 2: Use subject pronouns as predicate pronouns following a form of the linking verb be. Like predicate nouns, predicate pronouns rename the subject. Forms of the verb be include am, is, are, was, were, should be, has been, was being.

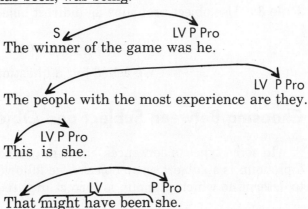

        S   LV P Pro
        The winner of the game was he.

                                 LV P Pro
        The people with the most experience are they.

                  LV P Pro
        This is she.

                        LV   P Pro
        That might have been she.

Object Pronouns

Study the following chart of **object pronouns.**

	Singular	**Plural**
1st Person	me	us
2nd Person	you	you
3rd Person	him, her, it	them

Characteristics of Object Pronouns

Notice that, like subject pronouns, object pronouns may be singular or plural. They may also refer to the person(s) speaking, the person(s) spoken to, or the person(s) or thing(s) spoken about.

Notice that the third person singular object pronouns include one that is masculine in gender (him), one that is feminine in gender (her), and one that can be used for objects and animals (it). The third person plural object pronoun, them, may be used to refer to plural nouns that are masculine, feminine, or both. Them can refer to people, animals, or things.

Using Object Pronouns Correctly

Rule 1: Use object pronouns as objects of the preposition (see Skill Unit 8).

> She gave the money to me.
>
> I went with them.

Rule 2: Use object pronouns as direct objects (see Skill Unit 9).

> She likes him.
>
> Please help her.

Rule 3: Use object pronouns as indirect objects (see Skill Unit 9).

> She gave us the money.
>
> We asked her a question.

Choosing Between Subject and Object Pronouns

In some types of sentences, there may be confusion about whether a pronoun is a subject or an object. The following examples show ways to determine which pronoun is correct in three common situations.

(1) Pronouns in Compound Subjects and Objects

In a compound subject or object, use the same pronoun you would use if the pronoun by itself were the subject or object. Look at the following sentence.

Mary and he/him are late.

This sentence needs a pronoun that can be part of the subject, so choose the subject pronoun <u>he</u>. <u>Mary and he</u> is the subject of the sentence.

To help you make the right choice, you can separate the two parts of the compound subject.

<u>Mary</u> is late.

<u>He</u> is late.

<u>Mary and he</u> are late.

When you separate the subjects this way, it is clear that <u>he</u> is the right choice.

Look at the next sentence.

We will invite Mary and he/him.

This sentence needs a pronoun to be part of the direct object, so choose the object pronoun <u>him</u>.

We will invite <u>Mary</u>.

We will invite <u>him</u>.

We will invite <u>Mary and him</u>.

Again, when you separate the two parts of the compound object, it is clear that <u>him</u> is the right choice.

Now try this one:

They told Mary and he/him the truth.

This sentence needs an indirect object, so choose the object pronoun <u>him</u>. Once again, separating the parts of the compound object will help you make the correct choice.

They told <u>Mary</u> the truth.

They told <u>him</u> the truth.

They told <u>Mary and him</u> the truth.

Try the sentence on the following page.

I took a ride with Mary and he/him.

This sentence needs an object of the preposition, so choose the object pronoun <u>him</u>. Once again, separating the parts of the compound can help you choose the correct pronoun.

I took a ride with <u>Mary</u>.

I took a ride with <u>him</u>.

I got a ride with <u>Mary and him</u>.

You will sometimes see a sentence in which a compound predicate pronoun follows a linking verb. The type of pronoun to use as a predicate pronoun is a subject pronoun:

The ushers were <u>he</u> and <u>I</u>.

Although it is correct, the use of subject pronouns after a linking verb somehow "just doesn't sound right" to most people. To determine which pronouns are correct in such a sentence, you may find it helpful to change the order of the parts of the sentence:

<u>He</u> and <u>I</u> were ushers.

When you do this, it is clear that <u>he</u> and <u>I</u> are correct.

(2) Pronouns After <u>Than</u> and <u>As</u>
Look at the following sentence:

She earns more money than I/me.

You might think that <u>me</u> was the correct choice because it "sounds right." However, this is what the sentence really means:

She earns more money than I/me earn.

When the sentence is written this way, you can see that <u>I</u> is the correct choice.
Look at the next sentence.

They are as happy as we/us.

Again there are missing words. This is what the sentence means:

They are as happy as we/us are.

When the sentence is written this way, it is clear that <u>we</u> is the correct choice.
Now look at this sentence.

They visit me more often than she/her.

Which pronoun is correct? It depends on what you mean to say. The sentence has two possible meanings:

> They visit me more often than she/her   (visits me).

> They visit me more often than   (they visit)   she/her.

The first sentence needs a subject. If that was the thought you wished to communicate, you would choose the subject pronoun <u>she</u>.

The second sentence needs a direct object. If that was the thought you wished to communicate, you would choose the object pronoun <u>her</u>.

Remember to fill in the missing words in any sentence containing <u>than</u> or <u>as</u>. Then choose the correct pronoun.

(3)   <u>We</u> and <u>Us</u> Followed by a Noun

Sometimes the pronouns <u>we</u> and <u>us</u> are followed by a noun that names who <u>we</u> or <u>us</u> are. In that case, ignore the noun and choose the pronoun you would use if there were no noun following it.

> We / Us workers need a raise.

Cross out the noun following the pronoun and the choice is clear.

> <u>We</u>/Us ~~workers~~ need a raise.

Now look at this example:

> You should pay we/us workers better.

Again, cross out the noun following the pronouns and the choice is clear.

> You should pay we/<u>us</u> ~~workers~~ better.

Apply what you have learned by doing the following exercise.

Exercise for Subskill 10A

Underline the correct pronoun in each sentence. In the blank, write whether the pronoun is used as a subject, predicate pronoun, direct object, indirect object, or object of the preposition.

EXAMPLE: The player with the most hits was <u>he</u>/him.

   <u>predicate pronoun.</u>

1.   (He/Him) and (I/me) are cousins.

2. I learned the news from Sandy and (he/him).

    _____

3. Tell Nancy and (they/them) that funny story.

    _____

4. I run faster than (she/her).

    _____

5. The losers were Terry and (I/me).

    _____

6. They taught (we/us) beginners some new dance steps.

    _____

7. (We/Us) beginners need lots of help and encouragement.

    _____

8. This is (she/her).

    _____

9. I like Becky more than (he/him).
    (meaning: I don't like him as much as I like Becky.)

    _____

10. I like Becky more than (he/him).
    (meaning: He doesn't like Becky as much as I do.)

    _____

Check your answers on pages 37 and 38 in the Answer Key for Book Two. If you correctly answered all 10 items, go to Subskill 10B. If not, do the Supplemental Exercise for Subskill 10A.

Supplemental Exercise for Subskill 10A

Review the information about subject and object pronouns on pages 191–197. Then do the following exercise.

Underline the correct pronoun in each sentence. In the blank, write whether the pronoun is used as a subject, predicate pronoun, direct object, indirect object, or object of the preposition.

EXAMPLE: Address the card to (she/her) and Joe.

_____ object of the preposition _____

1. He eats more slowly than (I/me).

   _____

2. Bring Marsha and (I/me) some ice cream.

   _____

3. (He/Him) and (she/her) are still together.

   _____

4. That must have been (they/them).

   _____

5. I see Ann and (he/him) over there.

   _____

6. We liked the movie better than (they/them).
   (meaning: They didn't like the movie as much as we did.)

   _____

7. He wants to sit between you and (I/me).

   _____

8. The best dancers in the room are (he/him) and (she/her).

   _____

9. (We/Us) renters need a break.

   _____

10. They are as sorry about it as (we/us).

   _____

Check your answers on page 38 in the Answer Key for Book Two. If you correctly answered 8 of 10 items, go to Subskill 10B. If not, ask your instructor for help.

Subskill 10B: Using Interrogative and Relative Pronouns Correctly

When you complete this subskill, you will be able to use the pronouns <u>who</u>, <u>whom</u>, <u>whose</u>, <u>that</u>, <u>which</u>, and <u>what</u> correctly.

Identifying Interrogative and Relative Pronouns

When the pronouns <u>who</u>, <u>whom</u>, <u>whose</u>, <u>which</u>, and <u>what</u> are used to ask questions, they are called **interrogative pronouns.**

<u>Who</u> are you?

<u>What</u> does he want?

<u>Whom</u> do you wish to see?

<u>Whose</u> sweater is that?

<u>Which</u> of the men is the tallest?

The pronouns <u>who</u>, <u>whom</u>, <u>whose</u>, <u>which</u>, and <u>that</u> can be used to introduce a subject-verb combination that describes another word (a noun) in the sentence. When they are used in this way, they are called **relative pronouns.**

The man [who bought the coat] paid cash.

<u>Who bought the coat</u> is a subject-verb combination used to describe the noun <u>man</u>. <u>Who</u> is the relative pronoun.

The woman [to whom he is speaking] is his sister-in-law.

<u>To whom he is speaking</u> is a subject-verb combination used to describe the noun <u>woman</u>. <u>Whom</u> is the relative pronoun.

The people [whose dog was lost] offered a reward.

<u>Whose dog was lost</u> is a subject-verb combination used to describe the noun <u>people</u>. <u>Whose</u> is the relative pronoun.

The package, [which the mail carrier delivered], was crushed.

<u>Which the mail carrier delivered</u> is a subject-verb combination used to describe the noun <u>package</u>. <u>Which</u> is the relative pronoun.

The coat [that I wanted] had already been sold.

<u>That I wanted</u> is a subject-verb combination used to describe the noun <u>coat</u>. <u>That</u> is the relative pronoun.

Using Interrogative and Relative Pronouns Correctly

Some words may be either interrogative pronouns or relative pronouns depending on how they are used in a sentence. The following examples will show you how to use these words as interrogative pronouns and relative pronouns.

"That," "Which," "Who," and "Whom"

<u>That</u> and <u>Which</u> should be used to refer only to animals or things.
<u>Who</u> and <u>Whom</u> should be used to refer only to people.

EXCEPTION: That is occasionally used to refer to people. However, who and whom are the preferred pronouns to use in referring to people.

CORRECT: The woman who lives next door is moving.

CORRECT BUT
NOT PREFERRED: The woman that lives next door is moving.

INCORRECT: The woman which lives next door is moving.

CORRECT: The dog to which she gave the bone is a German shepherd.

INCORRECT: The dog to whom she gave the bone is a German shepherd.

CORRECT: The dog that has the bone is a German shepherd.

INCORRECT: The dog who has the bone is a German shepherd.

"What"

What should not be used to introduce a descriptive subject-verb combination.

CORRECT: What is the matter?

INCORRECT: The person what I saw was very tall.

CORRECT: The person whom I saw was very tall.

"Whose"

Whose should be used to refer to people or animals, but not to things.

CORRECT: The man whose leg was broken was taken to the hospital.

CORRECT: The dog whose leg was broken was taken to the veterinarian's office.

INCORRECT: The lamp whose cord was frayed needed to be fixed.

NOTE: You can rewrite the last sentence correctly in several ways.

The lamp with the frayed cord needed to be fixed.

The frayed cord on the lamp needed to be fixed.

NOTE: You will learn more about whose and its sound-alike who's in Subskill 10D.

"Who" and "Whom"

Who is a subject pronoun. Whom is an object pronoun. To figure out which word to use, you must decide what function the pronoun has in the question or the descriptive subject-verb combination in which it appears. If the question or subject-verb combination needs a subject, choose who. If the question or subject-verb combination needs an object, choose whom.

Look at the following question.

S   V   DO
Who/Whom called you?

This question needs a subject for the verb called. Choose the subject pronoun who.

Look at the next question.

Who/Whom did you call?

To figure out which word you need in this question, first rewrite it as a statement.

S   V   DO
You did call who/whom

Now you can see that you is the subject and did call is the verb. The sentence needs a direct object. Choose the object pronoun whom.

The next example is more difficult to solve.

Who/Whom do you think is coming?

You might make the wrong choice in this sentence unless you cross out the words do you think right away. Once you do that, you will see that you need a subject for the verb is coming. Choose the subject pronoun who.

S
Who/Whom <s>do you think</s> is coming?

Now look at this sentence.

To who/whom did you give the package?

The sentence clearly needs an object of the preposition, so choose whom.

How about this one?

Who/whom did you give the package to?

This is basically the same sentence as the last one, except that the object has been separated from the preposition. Choose the object preposition whom.

Study the following examples of objects that have been separated from their prepositions.

<u>Whom</u> is it for?

The prepositional phrase is <u>for whom</u>.

<u>Whom</u> are you going with?

The prepositional phrase is <u>with whom</u>.

When words such as <u>do you think</u>, <u>did you say</u>, <u>did she believe</u>, or <u>does he think</u> appear in the middle of a question, cross out the words before choosing between <u>who</u> and <u>whom</u>.

Now look at this sentence with a descriptive subject-verb combination.

She is the person [who/whom won first prize.]

When <u>who</u> or <u>whom</u> is used in a descriptive subject-verb combination, ignore all the other words in the sentence and decide what function who/whom has in the subject-verb combination itself. This is the descriptive subject-verb combination in the above sentence:

    S   V   DO
who/whom won first prize

The verb is <u>won</u>. The combination needs a subject, so choose the subject pronoun <u>who</u>. Look at the next sentence:

He is the person [who/whom she met last night.]

The descriptive subject-verb combination is as follows:

        S   V
who/whom she met last night

The verb in the combination is <u>met</u>. The subject is <u>she</u>. What is missing is a direct object. Choose the object pronoun <u>whom</u>.

      S   V   DO
she met whom last night

Now look at this sentence:

The person [to who/whom I gave the package] was an employee.

The descriptive subject-verb combination is as follows:

to who/whom I gave the package

The combination can be rewritten as follows:

$$\overset{\text{S\ \ \ V}}{\text{I gave the package}} \text{ to } \overset{\text{O Prep}}{\text{who/whom.}}$$

You need an object of the preposition <u>to</u>. Choose the object pronoun <u>whom</u>.

NOTE: Ignore interrupters such as <u>I think</u>, <u>I believe</u>, <u>he said</u>, and <u>she thought</u> when choosing the correct pronoun in a descriptive subject-verb combination.

The man [who/whom I think is the best coach] is Landry.

The descriptive subject/verb combination is as follows:

who/whom I think is the best coach

The words <u>I think</u> are interrupters. Cross them out and the descriptive subject-verb combination becomes the following:

$$\overset{\text{S}}{\text{who/whom}} \ \text{I think} \ \overset{\text{V}}{\text{is}} \text{ the best coach}$$

This combination clearly needs a subject. Choose the subject pronoun <u>who</u>.

Apply what you have learned by doing the following exercise.

Exercise for Subskill 10B

Underline the correct pronoun in each sentence. If there are interrupters in the sentence, cross them out before making your choice.

EXAMPLE: <u>Who</u>/Whom is that?

1. (Who/Whom)   should I send the money to?
2. He is the man   (who/whom)   lives next door.
3. The horse   (who/that)   won the race is called Silver Streak.
4. (Who/Whom) do you think has the most points so far?
5. The player (who/which/what) caught the pass made a touchdown.
6. The person (who/whom) I think has the best plan is Ted.
7. The kitten with (whom/which) I played has sharp claws.
8. He is the only one (who/whom) I can trust.
9. The people (who/whom) we met were very nice.
10. (Who/Whom) will the voters elect next fall?

Check your answers on page 38 in the Answer Key for Book Two. If you correctly answered all 10 items, go to Subskill 10C. If not, do the Supplemental Exercise for Subskill 10B.

Supplemental Exercise for Subskill 10B

Review the information about interrogative and relative pronouns on pages 199–204. Then do the following exercise.

Underline the correct pronoun in each sentence. If there are interrupters in the sentence, cross them out before making your choice.

EXAMPLE: (Who/Whom)   did she think would buy it?

1. He was the one   (who/whom)   she thought should pay for it.

2. (Who/Whom)   is the best player?

3. The person   (who/whom)   you want is not here now.

4. (Who/Whom)   may I say is calling?

5. With   (who/whom)   are you going?

6. The dog   (who/that/what)   I saw was brown and white.

7. The person   (who/which/what)   stole my car was arrested.

8. The dog for   (whom/which)   I bought the collar is missing.

9. Tell me   (who/whom)   is singing that song.

10. (Who/Whom)   did you say I should call?

Check your answers on page 38 in the Answer Key for Book Two. If you correctly answered 8 of 10 items, go to Subskill 10C. If not, ask your instructor for help.

Subskill 10C: Using Demonstrative and Reflexive/Intensive Pronouns Correctly

When you complete this subskill, you will be able to use the **demonstrative pronouns** this, that, these, and those correctly. You will also be able to use the **reflexive/intensive pronouns** myself, yourself, himself, herself, ourselves, yourselves, and themselves correctly.

Demonstrative Pronouns

The **demonstrative pronouns** this, that, these, and those **are used to point out persons or things.** These words can be used as modifiers before a noun or they can stand alone as subject, objects, and predicate pronouns. (As you learned in Subskill 10B, that can also be a relative pronoun that introduces a descriptive subject-verb combination.)

That shirt is dirty.

That modifies the noun shirt. It tells which one. Shirt is the subject of the sentence.

That is dirty.

That is the subject of the sentence.

Give me that.

That is a direct object.

The best seats are those.

Those is a predicate pronoun that renames the subject seats.

Using Demonstrative Pronouns

(1) This and these are used to point out things nearby. Use this to point out one item and these to point out more than one. Because this and these are used only for items nearby, you don't need to use the word here after them. Never say this here or these here.

     CORRECT: This is mine.

     CORRECT: These are mine.

     INCORRECT: This here is mine.

     INCORRECT: These here are mine.

(2) That and those are used to point out things far away. That is used to point out one item. Those is used to point out more than one. Because that and those are used only for items far away, you don't need to use the word there after them. Never say that there or those there.

     CORRECT: That is a police car behind us.
                  Those are police cars behind us.

     INCORRECT: That there is a police car behind us.
                  Those there are police cars behind us.

(3) Use the singular modifiers this and that with the singular nouns kind and sort. Use the plural modifiers these and those with the plural nouns kinds and sorts.

CORRECT: I like <u>this kind</u> of shoe.

INCORRECT: I like <u>these kind</u> of shoes.

You are talking about only one kind—perhaps sandals.

CORRECT: I like <u>these kinds</u> of shoes.

The speaker is talking about more than one kind—perhaps sandals and loafers.

(4)   Never use the object pronoun <u>them</u> to point out.

CORRECT: <u>Those</u> are the ones I like.

INCORRECT: <u>Them</u> are the ones I like.

Reflexive/Intensive Pronouns

The reflexive/intensive pronouns all end in <u>self</u> or <u>selves</u>. Study the following chart.

	Singular	**Plural**
1st Person	myself	ourselves
2nd Person	yourself	yourselves
3rd Person	himself, herself, itself	themselves

The reflexive/intensive pronouns are often misspelled. Study the spelling of these pronouns carefully. Notice that each pronoun is spelled as one word. Notice that the singular pronouns end in <u>self</u> and the plural pronouns end in <u>selves</u>. Also notice that there are no such words as <u>hisself</u> or <u>theirselves</u>. The correct forms are <u>himself</u> and <u>themselves</u>. Before going any further, memorize the spellings of the reflexive/intensive pronouns.

Using Reflexive/Intensives Correctly

Reflexive/intensive pronouns are used in two different ways. They are used reflexively to show that a direct object, indirect object, or object of the preposition names the same person or thing as the subject. Often they show the subject doing something to the subject.

I cut myself.

They disqualified themselves.

He should give himself a chance.

When the pronouns are used intensively, they give emphasis to a noun or another pronoun, as in the examples on the following page.

I myself didn't understand the decision at all.

Even Barbara herself admitted she had made a mistake.

You yourself can see how much things have improved.

NOTE: Do not use reflexive/intensives where a subject or object pronoun is needed.

CORRECT: Jack and I worked hard.

INCORRECT: Jack and myself worked hard.

CORRECT: They thanked Jack and me for our efforts.

INCORRECT: They thanked Jack and myself for our efforts.

CORRECT: Give the papers to Jack and me.

INCORRECT: Give the papers to Jack and myself.

Apply what you have learned about demonstrative pronouns and reflexive/intensive pronouns by doing the following exercise.

Exercise for Subskill 10C

Underline the correct word or words in parentheses.

EXAMPLE: Do you enjoy (this sort of movie, these sort of movies)?

1.   He (himself, hisself) said there was a problem.

2.   (This, This here) is my friend Jerry.

3.   They are only hurting (themselves, theirselves).

4.   (Them, Those) are my shoes.

5.   We asked (ourself, ourselves) some tough questions after the accident.

6.   (Those there, Those) buildings are in bad shape.

7.   I like (that kind of program, those kind of programs).

8.   She's coming along with Tony and (myself, me).

9.   We often buy (that two kinds, those two kinds) of ice cream.

10.   Ralph and (yourself, you) know all the answers.

Check your answers on page 38 in the Answer Key for Book Two. If you correctly answered all 10 items, go to Subskill 10D. If not, do the Supplemental Exercise for Subskill 10C.

Supplemental Exercise for Subskill 10C

Review the information about demonstrative pronouns and reflexive/intensive pronouns on pages 205–208. Then do the following exercise.

Underline the correct word or words in parentheses.

EXAMPLE: I use (<u>those</u>, that) two kinds of screwdrivers.

1. (That there, That) tire is flat.

2. (Those, Them) are the ones I want.

3. They did all the work (theirselves, themselves).

4. Stan and (myself, I) are planning a trip.

5. He likes to work by (hisself, himself).

6. (These, These here) tools make the job a lot easier.

7. Do you enjoy (these kind of puzzles, this kind of puzzle)?

8. They are inviting Harry and (yourself, you).

9. We tried it (ourselves, ourself).

10. We went with Jim and (her, herself).

Check your answers on pages 38 and 39 in the Answer Key for Book Two. If you correctly answered 8 of 10 items, go to Subskill 10D. If not, ask your instructor for help.

Subskill 10D: Using Possessive Pronouns, Their Contraction Sound-Alikes, and Indefinite Pronouns Correctly

When you complete this subskill, you will be able to spell possessive pronouns correctly. You will know when to use a possessive pronoun and when to use a contraction sound-alike. You will also be able to choose the correct possessive pronoun to use after an indefinite pronoun.

Possessive Pronouns

You know that nouns may show possession.

Those keys belong to John.
Those are <u>John's</u> keys.
Those keys are <u>John's</u>.

Those keys belong to Betty.
Those are <u>Betty's</u> keys.
Those keys are <u>Betty's</u>.

Personal pronouns can also show possession.

Those keys belong to him.

Those are <u>his</u> keys.

Those keys are <u>his</u>.

Those keys belong to her.

Those are <u>her</u> keys.

Those keys are <u>hers</u>.

Some **possessive pronouns** are used as modifiers. Study the following chart.

	Singular	Plural
1st Person	my	our
2nd Person	your	your
3rd Person	his, her, its	their

Other possessive pronouns stand alone.

	Singular	Plural
1st Person	mine	ours
2nd Person	yours	yours
3rd Person	his, hers	theirs

That is <u>my</u> umbrella.
That is <u>mine</u>.

That is <u>their</u> car.
That is <u>theirs</u>.

You can borrow <u>his</u> bike.
You can borrow <u>his</u>.

Is this <u>her</u> pen.
Is this <u>hers</u>?

You learned another possessive pronoun in Subskill 10B. <u>Whose</u> is the possessive form of the pronouns <u>who</u> and <u>whom</u>.

<u>Who</u> owns that bicycle?

To <u>whom</u> does that bicycle belong?

<u>Whose</u> bicycle is that?

Study the spelling of all the possessive pronouns carefully, before going any further. Notice that, unlike possessive nouns, possessive pronouns do not contain apostrophes.

Contraction Sound-Alikes

Contractions are shortened forms of two or more words in which a letter or letters have been left out. An apostrophe is used to show where letters have been left out. The following contractions sound exactly like possessive pronouns and are often confused with them.

you're	=	you are	sounds like	your	=	belonging to you
it's	=	it is	sounds like	its	=	belonging to it
they're	=	they are	sounds like	their	=	belonging to them
there's	=	there is	sounds like	theirs	=	belonging to them
who's	=	who is	sounds like	whose	=	belonging to whom

Indefinite Pronouns

Indefinite pronouns are pronouns that do not refer to any specific person(s) or thing(s). Sometimes they refer to a group or quantity of persons or things.

<u>Somebody</u> sounded the alarm.
<u>Nothing</u> is wrong.
<u>Both</u> were right.
<u>Everybody</u> needs a chance.
<u>Many</u> of the pieces were missing.

Some indefinite pronouns are always singular, some are always plural, and others can be either singular or plural. Look at the following chart of indefinite pronouns:

Indefinite Pronouns

Singular			Plural	Singular or Plural
one	somebody	each	both	all
someone	everybody	another	several	most
everyone	anybody	either	many	some
anyone	nobody	neither	few	none
no one	nothing			

The pronouns in the third column of the chart are singular when they refer to part of one whole thing. They are plural when they refer to a number of things that you can count.

All of the cake is gone.   None of the cake has been eaten.

All of the guests are gone.   None of the members have voted yet.

Using Indefinite Pronouns with Possessives

You will often see sentences in which a possessive pronoun follows and refers to an indefinite pronoun. First, look at these sentences in which the possessive pronouns refer to a singular or plural noun.

The man is wearing his helmet.

The men are wearing their helmets.

It is clear that the first sentence requires the singular pronoun his because it refers to one man. It is clear that the second sentence requires the plural pronoun their because it refers to more than one man.

Now look at these sentences.

One of the men is wearing his helmet.

Each of the men is wearing his helmet.

Both of the men are wearing their helmets.

All of the men are wearing their helmets.

In these sentences, the indefinite pronouns are the antecedents of the possessive pronouns. That means that the indefinite pronouns are the words that the possessive pronouns refer to.

Pronouns must always agree in number, gender, and person with their antecedents. That means that the pronoun and the antecedent must match. If the antecedent is singular, the pronoun that refers to it must be singular. If the antecedent is plural, the pronoun that refers to it must be plural. If the antecedent is masculine, the pronoun that refers to it must be masculine. If the antecedent is feminine, the pronoun that refers to it should be feminine. If the antecedent is in the third person, the pronoun that refers to it should be in the third person.

One of the men is wearing his helmet.

In the sentence above, it is easy to see that the indefinite pronoun one is singular because it refers to one man. It is also easy to see that one is masculine in this sentence because it refers to a man. Indefinite pronouns are always in the third person. Therefore, the third person singular masculine pronoun his is used to refer to one.

The next sentence is more of a problem.

Each of the men is wearing his helmet.

It is clear that <u>each</u> needs a third person masculine pronoun to follow it. However, you may need to look back at the charts to remember that <u>each</u> is always singular, even though the sentence refers to more than one man.

Both of the men are wearing their helmets.

The sentence above uses the plural possessive because <u>both</u> is always plural.

All of the men are wearing their helmets.

Remember from the chart that <u>all</u> can be either singular or plural, depending on the noun that follows it. In this case, the noun that follows <u>all</u> is plural (<u>men</u>), so the plural possessive pronoun <u>their</u> is used.

Singular Indefinite Pronouns and Gender

Look at these sentences.

One of the men left his umbrella here.

One of the women left her umbrella here.

The gender required for each possessive pronoun is clear from clues in the sentences. Now look at this sentence.

Someone left _____ umbrella here.

You know from the chart that someone is always singular, so you can't use <u>their</u> in the blank. But you don't know the gender of the <u>someone</u> who left the umbrella, so which pronoun should you choose? Traditionally, the masculine pronoun <u>his</u> has been used to refer to a singular antecedent whose gender is not known. In the next subskill, you will learn some ways around this problem. When you don't know the gender of a singular antecedent, one solution is to write <u>his or her</u> or <u>her or his</u>.

Look at the next sentence:

Everybody left _____ coat in the bedroom.

In informal usage, most of us would say <u>their coats</u>. However, <u>everybody</u> is a singular indefinite pronoun. Therefore, you must use another singular pronoun to refer to it.

Everybody left her or his coat in the bedroom.

Apply what you have learned by doing the following exercise.

Exercise for Subskill 10D

Part A.   Underline the correct possessive pronoun or contraction in each sentence.

EXERCISE: That sandwich is (<u>hers</u>, her's).

1.   (Whose, Who's)   book is that?

2.   (Its, It's)   too early to eat lunch.

3.   (Their, They're)   already ten minutes late.

4.   Is this   (yours, your's)?

5.   They lost   (their, they're)   tickets.

6.   (Whose, Who's)   coming with me?

7.   You can borrow   (ours, our's).

8.   The bird hurt   (its, it's)   wing.

9.   (Your, You're)   right about him.

10.   I like   (his's, his)   the best.

11.   (Your, You're)   answer is right.

12.   (Theirs, Their's, There's)   something wrong with him.

13.   Is that   (theirs, their's, there's)?

14.   (Your, You're)   the best swimmer in the class.

15.   (Its, It's)   my turn.

Part B.   Underline the correct possessive pronoun in each sentence. Then draw an arrow to the indefinite pronoun it refers to. Use the strict rules of Standard English.

EXAMPLE: One of the women lost (<u>her</u>, their) purse.

16.   Has everybody finished   (his, their, her or his)   dinner?

17.   Both of the girls had already bought   (her ticket, their tickets).

18.   Neither of the girls had bought   (her ticket, their tickets).

19.   Each of the boys tried   (his, their)   best.

20.   Many of the boys tried   (his, their)   best.

Check your answers on page 39 in the Answer Key for Book Two. If you correctly answered all 20 items, go to Subskill 10E. If not, do the Supplemental Exercise for Subskill 10D.

Supplemental Exercise for Subskill 10D

Review the information about possessive pronouns, contraction sound-alikes, and indefinite pronouns on pages 209–214. Then do the following exercise.

Part A. Underline the correct possessive pronoun or contraction in each sentence.

EXAMPLE: Let's use (his's, <u>his</u>).

1. (Their, They're) going home now.

2. Is that (hers, her's)?

3. (Your, You're) hair looks good.

4. (Whose, Who's) going to help us?

5. The voters have made (their, they're) choice.

6. (Theirs, There's) cost more than (ours, our's).

7. (Your, You're) not sorry, are you?

8. (Whose, Who's) gloves are these?

9. (Its, It's) a shame.

10. The dog has broken (its, it's) leg.

Part B. Underline the correct possessive pronoun in each sentence. Then draw an arrow to the indefinite pronoun it refers to. Use the strict rules of Standard English.

EXAMPLE: Both of the men wore (his jacket, <u>their jackets</u>).

11. Each of the workers did (his, his or her, their) best.

12. A few of the workers did (his, his or her, their) best.

13. One of the women did (her, their) best.

14. Most of the women did (her, their) best.

15. Has anyone lost (his, his or her, their) wallet?

Check your answers on pages 39 and 40 in the Answer Key for Book Two. If you correctly answered 12 of 15 items, go to Subskill 10E. If not, ask your instructor for help.

Subskill 10E: Making Pronouns Agree With Their Antecedents

When you complete this subskill, you will be able to use pronouns correctly so that they agree with their antecedents in person, number, and gender.

As you learned in Subskills 10A and 10D, the antecedent of a pronoun is the word the pronoun refers to or stands in for. The antecedent may be one or more nouns, another pronoun, or a noun and a pronoun together.

James was tying his shoes.

The pronoun his refers to the antecedent James.

Ask your friend if she wants to contribute.

The pronoun she refers to the antecedent friend.

When Bill and I got home, we listened to the radio.

The pronoun we refers to the antecedent Bill and I.

Nancy and Hal spent all their money.

The pronoun their refers to the antecedents Nancy and Hal.

They spent all their money.

The pronoun their refers to the antecedent they.

As you learned in Subskill 10D, a pronoun must match or agree with its antecedent. Pronouns must agree with their antecedents in person, number, and gender.

Pronouns Must Agree with Their Antecedents in Person

If the antecedent is in the first person, the pronoun that refers to it should be in the first person. If the antecedent is in the second person, the pronoun that refers to it should also be in the second person. If the antecedent is in the third person, the pronoun that refers to it should also be in the third person.

I lost my pen.

The possessive pronoun my refers to the antecedent I. Both I and my are first person pronouns.

If Jenny and I work hard, we can accomplish a lot.

The first person pronoun we refers to the antecedent Jenny and I.

If you are lucky, your work will go smoothly.

The second person pronoun <u>your</u> refers to the second person antecedent <u>you</u>.

Pronouns Must Agree with Their Antecedents in Number

If the antecedent is singular, the pronoun that refers to it must be singular. If the antecedent is plural, the pronoun that refers to it must be plural.

The women cashed their paychecks.

The plural pronoun <u>their</u> refers to the plural antecedent <u>women</u>.

One of the women cashed her paycheck.

The singular pronoun <u>her</u> refers to the singular antecedent <u>one</u>.

A Third Person Singular Pronoun Must Agree with Its Antecedent in Gender

In the past, if the gender of a singular antecedent was unknown or was meant to refer to either men or women, a masculine pronoun was traditionally used. However, it is no longer considered acceptable to use <u>him</u> or <u>his</u> when a person of either gender might be meant.

One way to avoid this problem, as you have seen, is to write <u>her or his</u> (or <u>his or her</u>):

Everyone must make her or his own decisions.

Another solution is to use a plural antecedent, so that you can use the plural pronouns <u>they</u>, <u>them</u>, or <u>their</u>. That way, you can simply avoid the issue of gender.

Individuals must make their own decisions.

All persons must make their own decisions.

People must make their own decisions.

Other Issues in Pronoun-Antecedent Agreement

(1)   Antecedents Connected by <u>And</u>

When a pronoun refers to two or more antecedents connected by <u>and</u>, the pronoun should be plural.

The boy and the girl need their own books.

(2)   Antecedents Connected by <u>Or</u> or <u>Nor</u>

When a pronoun refers to two or more singular antecedents joined by <u>or</u> or <u>nor</u>, the pronoun should be singular.

Either Tim or Jerry will take his break now.

Neither Betty nor Jane could find her ticket.

When a pronoun refers to two or more plural antecedents joined by or or nor, the pronoun should be plural.

Either the men or the women will take their turns now.

When a pronoun refers to a singular antecedent and a plural antecedent joined by or or nor, the pronoun should agree with the antecedent that is closer to it. Since a plural pronoun will sound better, it's a good idea to place the plural antecedent last.

Neither Maria nor her daughters have finished their work.

Neither her daughters nor Maria has finished her work.

(3)   Pronouns That Refer to Collective Nouns

Some noun antecedents name a whole group or collection of people. These are called collective nouns. Collective nouns include team, jury, family, staff, audience, and squad.

When a group acts together, as one unit, it takes a singular pronoun.

The jury reached its decision.   (Together, the jury reached a single verdict.)

When the members of a group are acting as individuals, a collective noun takes a plural pronoun.

The jury cast their votes.   (Each member of the jury voted individually.)

In your own writing, you could revise this sentence to sound more natural:

The members of the jury cast their votes.

(4)   Interrupting Phrases

Ignore interrupting phrases that come between the antecedent and the pronoun. Phrases introduced by together with, along with, in addition to, as well as, and accompanied by are not part of the antecedent and should be ignored.

The coach, as well as the players, kept up his spirits.

(5) Indefinite Pronouns

Remember that some indefinite pronouns are always singular, some are always plural, and some can be either singular or plural, depending on the nouns that follow them. Review the charts on pages 210 and 211 and study the following examples.

They gave each of the children her or his allowance.

Neither of the students has received her or his test results.

Everybody took his or her turn.

Both of the girls forgot their umbrellas.

Most of the members have already cast their votes.

Most of the surface has already lost its shine.

Apply what you have learned by doing the following exercise.

Exercise for Subskill 10E

Underline the correct pronoun in parentheses. Circle its antecedent. Follow the rules of strict Standard English.

EXAMPLE: Neither Helen nor (Sue) could explain (her, their) reaction to the news.

1. If anyone wishes to leave early, (he, she or he, they) should see (his, her or his, their) supervisor.

2. When a person makes careful plans, (his or her, their, your) day goes more smoothly.

3. Both of the mothers brought (her baby, their babies) along.

4. The owner, as well as the employees, has (his or her, their) rights.

5. The employees, as well as the owner, have (his or her, their) rights.

6. The team won (its, their) first victory today.

7. The team changed into (its, their) uniforms quickly.

8. Neither Nick nor Kenny will lend me (his bike, their bikes).

9. Neither the owner nor the employees will change (his, his or her, their) positions.

10. The movie director and the famous actor did (his, their) best work together.

Check your answers on page 40 in the Answer Key for Book Two. If you answered all 10 items correctly, go to the Self-Check. If not, do the Supplemental Exercise for Subskill 10E.

Supplemental Exercise for Subskill 10E

Review the information about pronouns and antecedents on pages 216–219. Then do the following exercise.

Underline the correct pronoun in parentheses. Then circle its antecedent(s).

EXAMPLE: (Ralph and Larry) took   (his, <u>their</u>)   time.

1. Neither of the boys should give (his, their) statement until the attorney arrives.

2. When anyone arrives late,   (he, she or he, they)   should note the fact on (his, her or his, their) time slip.

3. Neither my father nor his brothers ever moved out of (his, their) old neighborhood.

4. If you see the dean or the registrar, tell   (her, them)   I am waiting.

5. The center and the guard did   (his, his or her, their)   best to win the game.

6. No one will be punished unless   (she violates, she or he violates, they violate)   a rule.

7. Most of the women did   (her, their)   work well.

8. Spanish, as well as English, should have   (its, their)   place in the curriculum.

9. At the next meeting, the committee will announce   (its, their)   decision.

10. When the committee meets tomorrow,   (it, they)   will discuss the issue.

Check your answers on page 40 in the Answer Key for Book Two. If you correctly answered 8 of 10 items, go to the Self-Check. If not, ask your instructor for help.

SELF-CHECK: SKILL UNIT 10

From each group of sentences, circle the letter of the sentence in which the pronoun does not follow the rules of Standard English. On the line provided, rewrite the incorrect sentence using Standard pronoun usage. If there is no error, circle letter e.

EXAMPLE: (a) Each brother had his own apartment.
          (b) Both methods have their merits.
          (c) Neither Henry nor Martin was wearing their watch.
          (d) Most people had had their dinner.

Neither Henry nor Martin was wearing his watch.

1. (a) The committee discussed their conflicting opinions.
    (b) He and I were losing, but we did not care.
    (c) You can see a slight resemblance between her and I.
    (d) The children hurt themselves while playing in the backyard.
    (e) No error.

2. (a) Most people have high opinions of themselves.
    (b) The winners were he and I.
    (c) Someone has left his or her shoes on the porch.
    (d) I like those kind of hubcaps.
    (e) No error.

3. (a) Is that him?
    (b) Leave the package with Ella and me.
    (c) To whom were you speaking on the telephone?
    (d) The dog had lost its bone.
    (e) No error.

4. (a) Bill is a friend whom I have not seen for many years.
    (b) The woman whom I met at the dance was a blonde.
    (c) She will give him and me the keys to the car.
    (d) Each of the workers may leave their job in an hour.
    (e) No error.

5. (a) Who did you give it to?
    (b) We women met for lunch yesterday.
    (c) He is better prepared than I.
    (d) The jury announced its verdict.
    (e) No error.

6. **(a)** That is the man to whom I spoke earlier.
   (b) Everybody has given her or his opinion on the question.
   (c) Whose going to the game with Jim and me?
   (d) Everybody left his or her books in the classroom.
   (e) No error.

7. **(a)** She handed Bill and myself our tickets.
   (b) It's certainly possible.
   (c) Is this yours?
   (d) If anyone wishes to leave early, she or he should see the supervisor.
   (e) No error.

8. **(a)** Sam is a man who I think is honest.
   (b) I like that kind of coat.
   (c) The bowling team has won its first championship.
   (d) Hank invited Bill and I on a fishing trip.
   (e) No error.

9. **(a)** It's supposed to snow tomorrow.
   (b) Neither of the candidates made their speech.
   (c) Whom did you meet in Topeka?
   (d) The sailor who fell overboard was rescued.
   (e) No error.

10. **(a)** The man whose dog was lost offered a reward.
    (b) Him and me drove downtown.
    (c) You yourself can see that the plan won't work.
    (d) These are men who should be rewarded.
    (e) No error.

11. **(a)** Are you as hungry as me?
    (b) The man who I think did the best job is Clint.
    (c) The general, as well as the troops, kept up his spirits.
    (d) Each of the trucks was assigned to its place.
    (e) No error.

12. **(a)** He did all the work hisself.
    (b) Those are yours, and these are mine.
    (c) Whose cat is this?
    (d) Give Susie and me all the money you have.
    (e) No error.

13. **(a)** Whom shall we see there?
    (b) Who do you think met me at the airport?
    (c) The movie that we saw last night was a comedy.
    (d) The woman who said hello to you is my aunt.
    (e) No error.

14. **(a)** Your making a big mistake.
    (b) The man to whom I gave the money disappeared.
    (c) No one should bring his or her lunch tomorrow?
    (d) Has everyone brought her or his own pen?
    (e) No error.

15. **(a)** Was it she who answered the telephone?
    (b) Were Dan and him at work yesterday?
    (c) Do those kinds of questions bother you?
    (d) Are these packages addressed to Dan and me?
    (e) No error.

16. **(a)** Is this her's?
    (b) Are they losing their minds?
    (c) John doesn't like this sort of camera.
    (d) Who's pitching tonight?
    (e) No error.

17. **(a)** It's bad news that my horse has broken its leg.
    (b) Give us workers a break.
    (c) The movie that we saw last night was a tragedy.
    (d) Them clothes need to be sent to the dry cleaners.
    (e) No error.

18. **(a)** They're taking some time off.
    (b) There's nothing wrong with that idea.
    (c) Both of the women paid cash for their purchases.
    (d) Give me some of that there candy.
    (e) No error.

19. **(a)** The manager told Bill and I that our work was above average.
    (b) We painted the house ourselves.
    (c) This house is ours.
    (d) The stray cat to which she had given some food came back again.
    (e) No error.

20. **(a)** The team invited their families to the game.
    (b) Who shall we take with us to the movie?
    (c) The decision pleased all of us except him.
    (d) He was angry when I mentioned his accident.
    (e) No error.

Check your answers on pages 40 and 41 in the Answer Key for Book Two. If you correctly answered 16 of 20 items, you have mastered these skills. If not, ask your instructor for help.

Posttest
GRAMMAR AND USAGE

The following test will help you find out how much you have learned about grammar and usage. The test will also help you to see which English skills you need to review.

The test is divided into ten parts, one part for each unit in the book. You may want to take the test all at once or one unit at a time, depending on what you and your instructor decide. When you complete the test, check your answers starting on page 41 in the Answer Key for Book Two. Then turn to the Skills Correlation Chart on page 244 in this book and circle the number of any questions you missed. The chart will show you which parts of this book covered the English skills that gave you the most trouble. You should review the parts that match the questions that you missed.

Skill Unit 1: Recognizing and Capitalizing Nouns

Part A. Underline all the nouns you find in the following sentences.

EXAMPLE: That large **book** is a **source** of great **wisdom.**

1. Brenda trained her dog to fetch the newspaper.

2. Are you cooking chicken and dumplings for dinner?

3. Rhode Island is the smallest state in the country.

4. His parents live in Atlanta.

Part B. Rewrite each sentence, capitalizing all the proper nouns you find.

EXAMPLE: Are you going home for thanksgiving?
Are you going home for Thanksgiving?

5. My appointment with dr. kennedy is on friday.

_____

6. My cousin kumar was offered a job with general motors in detroit, michigan.

_____

_____

7.   Her aunt marta's address is 1944 peach street.

_____

8.   He married sue ellen at st. mary's church in may, 1969.

_____

_____

Part C.   Read the following sentences carefully. Underline all the noun determiners you find and circle the nouns they signal.

EXAMPLE: **These** (shoes) are not supposed to be in **the** (middle) of **the (floor.)**

9.   Your friend gave me a ride to the library.

10.   The next time I see that dog, I'll call the police.

11.   Those people ordered a pizza.

12.   Their address is probably in the directory.

Part D.   Many of the nouns in the following sentences have special noun endings. Underline all the special noun endings you find.

EXAMPLE: Your coopera**tion** and generos**ity** are appreciated.

13.   This metal alloy has great durability and elasticity.

14.   This gift is in recognition of your years of service and dedication to the corporation.

15.   The reliability of this product is not recognized by the majority of customers.

16.   The computer is a modern appliance.

Part E.   Rewrite the following sentences, capitalizing all proper nouns.

EXAMPLE: "The best way to go," said my uncle mark, "is through central park."
             "The best way to go," said my Uncle Mark, "is through Central Park."

17.   My friend steve bates was elected senator from the fifth district.

_____

_____

18.   Three miles to the west, you'll find thayer avenue.

_____

_____

19. Shall we go to a mexican, italian, or chinese restaurant next
    saturday?

    _____

    _____

20. My mother always talks about her relatives in west germany and
    poland.

    _____

    _____

Skill Unit 2:   Using the Plural and Possessive Forms of Nouns

Part A.   Write the plural form for each noun given below.

EXAMPLE: foot _____**feet**_____

1. church   _____

2. baby   _____

3. donkey   _____

4. slacks   _____

5. child   _____

Part B.   Fill in the first blank in the following exercise using the singular possessive form of the noun. Fill in the second blank using the plural possessive form.

EXAMPLE: house   the _____**house's**_____ owner
           houses   the _____**houses'**_____ owners

6. glass   the _____ stem
   glasses   the _____ stems

7. friend   the _____ name
   friends   the _____ names

8. product   the _____ manufacturer
   products the _____ manufacturer

9. child   the _____ parents
   children the _____ parents

10. mouse   the _____ tail
    mice   the _____ tails

Part C.   In the spaces provided, write each noun you find in the following sentences and state whether it is singular, singular possessive, plural, or plural possessive.

EXAMPLE: That is Paul's tie.
Paul's—sing. poss.   tie—singular

11.   The child's temperature is 102 degrees.

_____

_____

12.   Her brothers' names are José and Miguel.

_____

_____

13.   Our mother's kitchen is always spotless.

_____

_____

14.   Men's and ladies' clothing is on the fourth level of the store.

_____

_____

15.   Please put the knives and forks in Ushi's basket.

_____

_____

Part D.   Underline the correct form of the word to complete each of the following sentences.

EXAMPLE: The dentist checked my   (**teeth's**, teeths', teethes')   alignment.

16.   My   (parents, parent's, parents')   own a home in Chicago.

17.   The   (supervisors, supervisor's, supervisors')   son was given the job I wanted.

18.   The lids on all the   (boxes, box's, boxes')   were open.

19.   The   (city's, cities, cities')   sanitation department is threatening to go on strike again.

20.   The   (tomato's, tomatoes, tomatoes')   don't look very good this week.

Skill Unit 3:   Reviewing Verbs

Part A.   Divide each sentence into two parts by drawing a line between the complete subject and the complete predicate. Then underline the simple subject once and the verb twice.

EXAMPLE: **<u>Randy</u>|<u>baked</u>** a cake last weekend.

1.   Our dog's name is Scruffy.

2.   Wendy is proud of her new office.

3.   The technician from the electric company fixed the problem.

4.   We really needed a vacation.

Part B.   In each pair of sentences below, the underlined word is used once as a noun and once as a verb. Write <u>N</u> next to the sentence with the underlined noun and <u>V</u> next to the sentence with the underlined verb.

EXAMPLE: _____**V**_____   Pam will <u>play</u> the part of Ophelia.
   _____**N**_____   *Hamlet* is an exciting <u>play</u>.

5 _____   <u>Help</u> me!
   _____   They gave us their <u>help</u>.

6.   _____   My <u>head</u> aches.
   _____   Does Gwen <u>head</u> the finance committee?

7.   _____   Scott made the long <u>drive</u> in three hours.
   _____   We often <u>drive</u> to Tulsa on the weekends.

8.   _____   The <u>sail</u> tore in the strong winds.
   _____   The ships <u>sail</u> tomorrow for Spain.

Part C.   Each of the following sentences contains a verb phrase. For each sentence, do the following:

· Underline all the words in the verb phrase.

· Write <u>HV</u> above the helping verbs.

· Write <u>MV</u> above the main verb of each sentence.

Review your work to be sure you have completed each step.

 HV   HV   MV
EXAMPLE: You **<u>should</u> <u>have</u> <u>called</u>** earlier.

9.   Ida does not drive to work.

10.   Harry may work on his brother's farm this summer.

11.   We have seen only half of the program.

12.   The suspect had been seen outside the bank.

Part D.   Each of the following sentences contains a linking verb or linking verb phrase. Underline the verb or verb phrase in each sentence.

EXAMPLE: The hikers **remained** cheerful despite the storm.

13.   Sara feels much better today.

14.   Gordon is an excellent cook.

15.   The lines should appear parallel.

16.   The girl grew impatient.

Part E.   Each of the following sentences contains a form of the verb <u>to be</u>. For each sentence, do the following:

- Underline the verb in each sentence and decide if the form of <u>to be</u> is used as a linking verb or if it is used as a helping verb in a verb phrase.

- Write <u>LV</u> in the blank if it is used as a linking verb.

- Write <u>HV</u> if the form of <u>to be</u> is used as a helping verb.

Review your work to be sure you have completed each step.

EXAMPLE: They <u>are trying</u> to hurry.   <u>**HV**</u>
Rudy <u>was</u> skeptical.   <u>**LV**</u>

17.   Melvin was a good student.   _____

18.   I am reading a funny book.   _____

19.   I am very pleased with your progress.   _____

20.   They could have been more friendly.   _____

Part F.   The following sentence pairs use the same words as linking and action verbs. Read each pair carefully. Decide which verb is used as an action verb and write <u>AV</u> in the space provided. Write <u>LV</u> next to the sentence in which the word is used as linking verb.

EXAMPLE: The tourists <u>looked</u> at the monument.   <u>**AV**</u>
The tourists <u>looked</u> enthusiastic.   <u>**LV**</u>

21.   The cook <u>tasted</u> the stew.   _____
It <u>tasted</u> worse than usual.   _____

22.   The roast <u>smelled</u> delicious.   _____
The children <u>smelled</u> the cake baking.   _____

23.   The plans <u>sounded</u> interesting.   _____
Gerry <u>sounded</u> the alarm immediately.   _____

Skill Unit 4:   Using Verb Tenses Correctly

Part A.   Fill in the blanks with the correct present tense form of the verb indicated.

EXAMPLE: Jeanie _____**pushes**_____ herself too hard and
                  push
_____**worries**_____ too much about her job.
      worry

1. Every afternoon Fred _____ his homework and
                                    do
_____ television.
    watch

2. The shirt _____ too much and_____
               cost   have
to be dry cleaned.

3. Kurt _____ the guitar and _____
           play   study
music.

Part B. Fill in the blanks with the correct past tense form of the verb indicated.

EXAMPLE: The fire _____**danced**_____ and_____**popped**_____
               dance   pop
cheerily.

4. We _____ for a place to park and finally
      look
_____ a space near the gate.
    find

5. Simon _____ to the door and_____
           hurry   try
to open it.

6. They _____ a table next to the windows but
      prefer
_____ one next to the door.
    take

Part C. Rewrite each of the following sentences twice. First change the verb to the future tense using <u>will</u>. Next change the verb to the future tense using <u>be</u> + <u>going to</u>.

EXAMPLE: Ken feels much better.
<u>Ken will feel much better.</u>
<u>Ken is going to feel much better.</u>

7. I am extremely sleepy.

_____

_____

8.   Oscar needs help with the packages.

_____

_____

9.   The neighbors hate Dana's loud music.

_____

_____

Part D.   Each of the following sentences is written in the past tense. On the lines provided, rewrite each sentence in the present perfect, the past perfect, and the future perfect tenses.

EXAMPLE: PAST: Warren had his lunch.
           PRES. PERF.:   Warren has had his lunch.
           PAST PERF.:   Warren had had his lunch.
           FUT. PERF.:   Warren will have had his lunch.

10.   PAST: Roberto received an answer.

      PRES. PERF.:   _____

      PAST PERF.:   _____

      FUT. PERF.:   _____

11.   PAST: Christina was sick for three days.

      PRES. PERF.:   _____

      PAST PERF.:   _____

      FUT. PERF.:   _____

12.   PAST: They did everything possible.

      PRES. PERF.:   _____

      PAST PERF.:   _____

      FUT. PERF.:   _____

Skill Unit 5:   Using Progressive Forms and Irregular Verbs

Part A.   In each of the following sentences, underline the correct helping verb of each pair in parentheses. Then fill in the blank with the progressive form of the verb in parentheses under the blank.

EXAMPLE: He (**will be,** was) _____**changing**_____ the locks tomorrow.   (change)

1. We   (are, had been) _____ the game when the
                                    (win)
    rain started.

2. I (have, am) _____ my hair now.
                        (wash)

3. Carl (will be, was) _____ his family for Thanks-
                                (visit)
    giving.

4. Joe could tell by the large puddles that it   (was, had been)
    _____ all night.
              rain

5. Daniel (was, will be) _____ to tie his shoe when
                                    stop
    the woman bumped into him.

Part B.   Fill in the blanks in the following with either the past or the past
participle form of the verb in parentheses.

EXAMPLE: I have _____**known**_____ Jerry for three years.   (know)

6. Mary had _____ on that airline several times be-
    fore. (fly)

7. Hope _____ the moon through the telescope.
    (see)

8. The meeting was _____ in the hall. (hold)

9. Barbara _____ the address Carol gave her. (lose)

10. I already _____ lunch. (eat)

Part C.   Above each of the following sentences are the principal parts
of one or two verbs. In each blank, write the verb form that correctly
completes each sentence.

EXAMPLE: let let let   leave   left   left
            Let me stay here.
            Leave me a couple of dollars.

11. learn   learned   learned   teach   taught   taught
     Our parents _____ us to be polite.
     We _____ our table manners early.

12. lie lay lain   lay laid laid

Valerie _____ the carpet on the floor.

Kevin _____ waiting for the alarm clock to go off.

13. sit sat sat   set set set

The cashier _____ the change on the counter.

We _____ waiting for hours.

Skill Unit 6:   Identifying Adjectives and Using Them Correctly

---

Part A.   Underline all of the adjectives you find in the following sentences.

EXAMPLE: Do you see the **tall** man in the **green** shirt?

1. Janet can fix our old, broken radio.

2. That swimming instructor taught many children to swim last summer.

3. Those old, abandoned buildings are not a safe playground.

4. Our German friends are coming over for a Mexican dinner tonight.

5. Some people think that all Dobermans are vicious dogs.

Part B.   Underline all the adjectives you find in the following sentences.

EXAMPLE: Maggie seems **restless** and **unhappy** today.

6. My father was a penniless Russian immigrant.

7. He brought only a few old clothes and five tattered books with him.

8. The house, large and cheerful, was perfect for our growing family.

9. Nicholas felt sad and depressed.

10. Her first child was a healthy, happy baby with blue eyes and blonde hair.

Part C.   Change the words given in parentheses into adjectives by adding one of the following endings: ible, able, ic, ous, ious, itious, less, al, ative, ive, and ful. Be sure to make any necessary spelling changes. Use a dictionary if you are in doubt.

EXAMPLE: Winston's sister is **superstitious.** (superstition)

11. The wedding was a _____ occasion for both families. (joy)

12. Margaret is an _____ child. (imagine)

13. Such _____ driving will lead to an accident. (care)

14. The shooting was _____. (accident)

15. The bed is not very _____. (comfort)

Part D. Fill in the blanks using the comparative and superlative forms of the adjectives given.

EXAMPLE: economical   This cut of meat is **more economical** than that one.
The flank steak is the **most economical** of all.

16. noisy   Randy is _____ than Mark.
He is the _____ boy in the entire class.

17. expensive   Meat is _____ this month than last.
It is the _____ it has been all year.

18. good   This method is _____ than Norman's.
It is the _____ method we could devise.

19. hot   This pot keeps the coffee _____ than our old pot.
It's the _____ coffee I've ever tried to drink.

20. comfortable   You won't find a chair that is _____ than this one.
It's the _____ chair made.

Skill Unit 7:   Identifying Adverbs and Using Them Correctly

Part A. Read the sentences on page 236 and do the following:

- Underline the adverbs you find.

- Draw an arrow to the word each adverb modifies.

- In the blank following the sentence, write How?, When?, How often?, Where?, or How much? to show which question the adverb answers about the word it modifies.

Review your work to make sure you have completed each step.

EXAMPLE: This coat is **too** small for me.   **How much?**

1.   Frances exercises daily.   _____

2.   Please drive carefully.   _____

3.   Eric keeps the collection there.   _____

4.   Tomorrow I will visit Ernie.   _____

Part B.   Expand the following sentences using the adverbs given in parentheses. Several different placements may be correct.

EXAMPLES: They drove the injured child to the hospital.   (immediately)

Each of the following answers is correct:

> Immediately they drove the injured child to the hospital.
> They drove the injured child immediately to the hospital.
> They drove the injured child to the hospital immediately.

I had a flat tire.   (first—I was the first to have a flat tire.)

The following is the only correct answer:

> I had a flat tire first.

5.   The driver closed his eyes.   (recklessly)

_____

_____

6.   She dances gracefully.   (quite)

_____

7.   I hated being alone.   (always—I was alone all the time.)

_____

_____

8.   I hated being alone.   (always—I hated it every time.)

_____

_____

Part C.   Use the adverb form of the underlined adjective used in the first sentence to complete the second sentence in each set.

EXAMPLE: The <u>heavy</u> rain pounded on the tin roof.
          The rain pounded   **heavily**   on the tin roof.

9.   The <u>greedy</u> cat eyed my bird.
     The cat eyed my bird   _____ .

10. He was a <u>fast</u> runner in high school.

He ran the 100-yard dash very _____ in high school.

11. Please be <u>honest</u> with me.

Look me in the eye and tell me _____ .

Part D. Fill in the blanks with the comparative and superlative forms of the adverb given.

EXAMPLE: long This movie is much _____**longer**_____ than the one we saw last week.

It is probably the _____**longest**_____ movie I have ever seen.

12.   fast   The cheetah runs _____ than the lion.

Of all the animals, the cheetah runs the

_____ .

13.   rapidly   Alan always finishes his homework assignments

_____ than I do.

Of all the students in our class, he finishes the

_____ .

14.   badly   I sing _____ than Julio.

But of all the choir members, Carlos sings the

_____ .

Part E. Read each of the sentence pairs below. Underline the word in parentheses that correctly completes each sentence.

EXAMPLE: Mary Jo looked   (**happy,** happily)   the last time I saw her.

Mary Jo looked   (happy, **happily**)   at the presents on the table.

15. The spaghetti tasted so   (good, well).

Hank cooks spaghetti really   (good, well).

16. Ralph looked   (frantic, frantically)   for the ring.

Ralph really looked   (frantic, frantically)   when he couldn't find it.

17. Angie looks   (terrible, terribly).

She must be   (terrible, terribly)   overworked.

Part F. Underline the word in the parentheses that correctly completes each sentence.

EXAMPLE: This meat is   (kind of, **somewhat**)   overcooked.

18. We didn't have   (nothing, anything)   to do with it.

19. I felt so   (bad, badly)   about the accident.

20. He did   (good, well)   on his final exams.

Skill Unit 8:   Using Prepositional Phrases as Modifiers

Part A.   Do the following for each of the sentences below:

· Underline all the prepositional phrases you find.

· Circle each preposition.

· Write OP above the object of each preposition.

Review your work to make sure that you have completed each step.

              OP   OP

EXAMPLE: (After) work, we met (at) the restaurant.

1.   On Friday, we are taking the children to the zoo.

2.   We'll take our lunch in a picnic basket.

3.   We'll find a spot on the grass under the trees.

4.   After lunch, we'll look at the animals in their cages.

5.   We'll watch the bears climbing on the rocks and swimming in their pool.

6.   We'll stand in front of the lions' cage and look carefully for the fish under the plants in the aquarium.

7.   We'll walk through the aviary and admire the birds from exotic places.

8.   Together with the children, we'll have a great time at the zoo.

Part B.

Part I.   Do the following for each of the sentences below:

· Underline all the prepositional phrases you find.

· Draw an arrow to the word each phrase modifies.

· In the blank, write <u>adjective</u> if the phrase modifies a noun or pronoun, and <u>adverb</u> if the phrase modifies the verb.

Review your work to make sure you have completed each step.

EXAMPLE: The cat **in the apple tree** belongs to me.
           adjective

9.   I knew the woman at the next table.   _____

10.   The little boy ran across the busy street.   _____

11.   Sheldon will be leaving in a while.   _____

12.   I won't leave without you.   _____

13.   We always read the paper after breakfast.   _____

14.   She was a friend of my mother.   _____

Part II.   In some of the following sentences, it is clear what the prepositional phrases are describing. In others, the placement of the phrases has confusing or even humorous results. If the meaning of a sentence is clear, write C in the blank. If the meaning is not clear, rewrite the sentence, changing the position of the prepositional phrase.

EXAMPLE: The Malloys saw several unusual animals on vacation in Australia.
<u>On vacation in Australia, the Malloys saw several unusual animals</u>.

15.   In spite of their finicky dispositions, many people own Siamese cats.

_____

_____

16.   Under the refrigerator, the dog could smell the rat.

_____

_____

17.   After the thunderstorm, we saw a beautiful rainbow.

_____

18.   With a flash of white tail, the hunters saw the deer leap into the forest.

_____

_____

19.   The skier raced down the hill with the orange jumpsuit.

_____

_____

20.   From the top of the flagpole, Henry watched the bird take flight.

_____

_____

Skill Unit 9:   Identifying Simple Sentence Patterns

Part A.   Each of the following sentences fits one of these basic sentence patterns:

Subject + Action Verb   (S + AV)
Subject + Action Verb + Direct Object   (S + AV + DO)
Subject + Action Verb + Indirect Object
    + Direct Object   (S + AV + IO + DO)

Identify the sentence type by writing the sentence pattern formula in the blank following the sentence.

EXAMPLE: Ellie gave me her favorite sweater. **S + AV + IO + DO**

1. Missy and I saw Marvin and Gail at the library yesterday.
    _____

2. Tony is going to buy me a coat for my birthday.
    _____

3. We often sit and talk on the porch in the evenings.
    _____

4. I already told my husband about your new job.
    _____

5. The concert lasted for three hours. _____

6. Martha gave me your new address. _____

Part B.   Each of the following sentences fits one of these basic sentence patterns:

Subject + Action Verb   (S + AV)
Subject + Action Verb + Direct Object   (S + AV + DO)
Subject + Action Verb + Indirect Object
    + Direct Object   (S + AV + IO + DO)
Subject + Linking Verb + Predicate Noun   (S + LV + PN)
Subject + Linking Verb + Predicate
    Adjective   (S + LV + PA)

Identify the sentence type by writing the pattern formula in the blank after each sentence.

EXAMPLE: The dinner proved well worthwhile.
              S + LV + PA

7. Kurt is becoming a very good ball player. _____

8. Nina practices two hours daily. _____

9. The food smells absolutely delicious. _____

10. It will be ready in about an hour. _____

11. I smell something burnt. _____

12. Aunt Meg and Uncle Cleo are coming to dinner tomorrow.
_____

13. Last time, Uncle Cleo told us a great story. _____

14. They are always the life of the party. _____

Part C. Read each of the following sentences carefully and do these three steps:

- Rewrite each sentence in usual order (subject + verb) on the lines provided.

- If the sentence has a subject that is understood, put the understood subject in parentheses in your rewritten version.

- Write S above each subject and V above each verb.

Review your work to make sure you have completed each step.

EXAMPLE: Wait!

         S   V
        (You) wait!

15. Do you need any help?

_____

_____

16. On the south shore of the lake is a cozy little restaurant.

_____

_____

17. Don't look!

_____

18. At the very end of the book is the solution to the mystery.

_____

_____

19. Here is my recipe for chocolate chip cookies.

_____

_____

20. Did you feed the dog last night?

_____

_____

Skill Unit 10:   Using Pronouns Correctly

Part A.   Underline the correct pronouns to complete each sentence.

EXAMPLE: (**He,** Him)   and   (**I,** me)   worked together in Boston.

1. We are as excited about it as   (they, them).

2. Our best friends are   (he, him)   and his wife.

3. Give   (I, me)   and   (they, them)   a chance to help   (he, him).

4. Did you see   (she, her)   or   (they, them)   at the movie last night?

Part B.   Underline the correct pronouns to complete each sentence.

EXAMPLE: (Who, **Whom**)   did you wish to see?

5. Are you sure this is the person   (who, whom)   you talked with?

6. He is the salesperson   (who, whom)   I think helped me.

7. (Who, Whom)   will we ask to go with us?

8. Sandy is one person   (who, that)   I don't think should go.

Part C.   Underline the correct pronouns to complete each sentence.

EXAMPLE: (These here, **These**)   are the only clothes I need.

9. Alex   (hisself, himself)   was responsible for the accident.

10. Do you sell   (these kinds, this kind, these kind)   of tools?

11. He and   (yourself, you)   are invited.

12. (This, This here)   car is very fast.

Part D.   Underline the correct word to complete each sentence.

EXAMPLE: There's the grocer   (who's, **whose**)   face seems familiar.

13. Each of our friends received   (her or his, they're, their)   invitation today.

14. I don't know   (whose, who's)   hat this is.

15. The baby bird   (who, that)   we found had fallen out of   (its, it's)   nest.

16. (We, Us)   workers have rights like   (your's, yours).

Part E. Underline the correct pronoun to complete each sentence.

EXAMPLE: Thelma, as well as her colleagues, refused to accept   (**her,** their)   new contract.

17.   Everyone forgot   (his or her, their)   uniform.

18.   Neither my grandfather nor his brothers ever lost   (his, their) heavy German accents.

19.   The president of the company, as well as her management staff, expressed   (her, their)   views on the new company policies.

20.   One of my sons already has   (his, their)   driver's license.

Skills Correlation Chart for Posttest

After you check your answers, look at the following chart. Circle the number of each question you missed. Then study the subskill in which the skills for the questions you missed are explained.

		QUESTION NUMBER	SUBSKILL NUMBER	SUBSKILL NAME	PAGE NUMBER
Skill Unit One	RECOGNIZING AND CAPITALIZING NOUNS	1 2 3 4	1A	Identifying Nouns	pages 24–26
		5 6 7 8	1B	Identifying Proper Nouns and Common Nouns	pages 26–30
		9 10 11 12	1C	Recognizing Noun Determiners	pages 30–32
		13 14 15 16	1D	Recognizing Noun Endings	pages 32–33
		17 18 19 20	1E	Other Capitalization Rules	pages 33–40

If you correctly answered 15 or fewer questions, you should review the subskills in Unit One for the questions you missed.
If you correctly answered 16 or more of the questions in Unit One, go to Skill Unit Two.

		QUESTION NUMBER	SUBSKILL NUMBER	SUBSKILL NAME	PAGE NUMBER
Skill Unit Two	USING THE PLURAL AND POSSESSIVE FORMS OF NOUNS	1 2 3 4 5	2A	Writing the Plural Forms of Nouns	pages 44–47
		6 7 8 9 10	2B	Writing the Possessive Forms of Nouns	pages 47–50
		11 12 13 14 15	2C	Recognizing Noun Forms	pages 50–53
		16 17 18 19 20	2D	Choosing the Correct Noun Form	pages 53–56

If you correctly answered 15 or fewer questions, you should review the subskills in Unit Two for the questions you missed.
If you correctly answered 16 or more of the questions in Unit Two, go to Skill Unit Three.

		QUESTION NUMBER	SUBSKILL NUMBER	SUBSKILL NAME	PAGE NUMBER
Skill Unit Three	REVIEWING VERBS	1 2 3 4	3A	Identifying Sentence Parts	pages 58–62
		5 6 7 8	3B	Recognizing Action Verbs	pages 62–64
		9 10 11 12	3C	Recognizing Verb Phrases	pages 65–68
		13 14 15 16	3D	Recognizing Linking Verbs	pages 68–71
		17 18 19 20	3E	Identifying Linking Verbs and Helping Verbs	pages 71–74
		21 22 23	3F	Identifying Linking Verbs and Action Verbs	pages 74–75

If you correctly answered 17 or fewer questions, you should review the subskills in Unit Three for the questions you missed.
If you correctly answered 18 or more of the questions in Unit Three, go to Skill Unit Four.

		QUESTION NUMBER	SUBSKILL NUMBER	SUBSKILL NAME	PAGE NUMBER
Skill Unit Four	USING VERB TENSES CORRECTLY	1 2 3	4A	Using Verbs Correctly in the Present Tense	pages 77–81
		4 5 6	4B	Using Verbs Correctly in the Past Tense	pages 81–84
		7 8 9	4C	Using Verbs Correctly in the Future Tense	pages 84–87
		10 11 12	4D	Using Past Participles to Form the Perfect Tenses	pages 88–92

If you correctly answered 9 or fewer questions, you should review the subskills in Unit Four for the questions you missed.
If you correctly answered 10 or more of the questions in Unit Four, go to Skill Unit Five.

		QUESTION NUMBER	SUBSKILL NUMBER	SUBSKILL NAME	PAGE NUMBER
Skill Unit Five	USING PROGRESSIVE FORMS AND IRREGULAR VERBS	1 2 3 4 5	5A	Using the Progressive Forms of Tenses Correctly	pages 95–101
		6 7 8 9 10	5B	Using the Past and Past Participle Forms of Irregular Verbs Correctly	pages 101–107
		11 12 13	5C	Using Some Problem Verbs Correctly	pages 107–113

If you correctly answered 9 or fewer questions, you should review the subskills in Unit Five for the questions you missed.
If you correctly answered 10 or more of the questions in Unit Five, go to Skill Unit Six.

		QUESTION NUMBER	SUBSKILL NUMBER	SUBSKILL NAME	PAGE NUMBER
Skill Unit Six	IDENTIFYING ADJECTIVES AND USING THEM CORRECTLY	1 2 3 4 5 6 7 8 9 10 11 12 13 14 15 16 17 18 19 20	6A 6B 6C 6D	Identifying Adjectives Locating Adjectives by Their Position in the Sentence Recognizing Adjectives by Their Endings Using Adjectives to Make Comparisons	pages 114–123 pages 124–128 pages 128–131 pages 131–136
		If you correctly answered 15 or fewer questions, you should review the subskills in Unit Six for the questions you missed. If you correctly answered 16 or more of the questions in Unit Six, go to Skill Unit Seven.			
Skill Unit Seven	IDENTIFYING ADVERBS AND USING THEM CORRECTLY	1 2 3 4 5 6 7 8 9 10 11 12 13 14 15 16 17 18 19 20	7A 7B 7C 7D 7E 7F	Identifying Adverbs Positioning Adverbs in a Sentence Forming Adverbs From Adjectives Using Adverbs to Make Comparisons Choosing Between Adjectives and Adverbs Usage Problems With Certain Adverbs	pages 138–143 pages 143–145 pages 145–149 pages 149–152 pages 152–155 pages 155–158
		If you correctly answered 15 or fewer questions, you should review the subskills in Unit Seven for the questions you missed. If you correctly answered 16 or more of the questions in Unit Seven, go to Skill Unit Eight.			
Skill Unit Eight	USING PREPOSITIONAL PHRASES AS MODIFIERS	1 2 3 4 5 6 7 8 9 10 11 12 13 14 15 16 17 18 19 20	8A 8B	Identifying Prepositional Phrases Using Prepositional Phrases Effectively	pages 161–165 pages 165–169
		If you correctly answered 15 or fewer questions, you should review the subskills in Unit Eight for the questions you missed. If you correctly answered 16 or more of the questions in Unit Eight, go to Skill Unit Nine.			
Skill Unit Nine	SIMPLE SENTENCE PATTERNS	1 2 3 4 5 6 7 8 9 10 11 12 13 14 15 16 17 18 19 20	9A 9B 9C	Identifying Action Verb Sentence Patterns Identifying Linking Verb Sentence Patterns Identifying the Sentence Parts of Special Sentences	pages 173–180 pages 180–184 pages 184–188
		If you correctly answered 15 or fewer questions, you should review the subskills in Unit Nine for the questions you missed. If you correctly answered 16 or more of the questions in Unit Nine, go to Skill Unit Ten.			
Skill Unit Ten	USING PRONOUNS CORRECTLY	1 2 3 4 5 6 7 8 9 10 11 12 13 14 15 16 17 18 19 20	10A 10B 10C 10D 10E	Using Subject and Object Pronouns Correctly Using Interrogative and Relative Pronouns Correctly Using Demonstrative and Reflexive/Intensive Pronouns Correctly Using Possessive Pronouns, Their Contraction Sound-Alikes, and Indefinite Pronouns Correctly Making Pronouns Agree With Their Antecedents	pages 191–199 pages 199–205 pages 205–209 pages 209–215 pages 216–220
		If you correctly answered 15 or fewer questions, you should review the subskills in Unit Ten for the questions you missed. If you correctly answered 16 or more of the questions in Unit Ten, go to Book Three.			